To Live & Write in Dixie

To Live & Write in Dixie

P.T. PAUL

Negative Capability PRESS

MOBILE, ALABAMA

Cover and Interior Design by Megan Cary

ISBN 978-0-942544-70-1
Library of Congress Control Number: 2010922203

Negative Capability Press
62 Ridgelawn Drive East
Mobile, Alabama 36608

(251) 591-2922
www.negativecapabilitypress.org

For Lillian, with thanks.

Acknowledgements

My thanks to the people who made this book possible:

Dr. Sue Walker

Frye Gaillard

Larry "Satch" Sampson

FOREWARD

P.T. Paul grew up Southern. She was raised in Whistler, just north of Mobile, the fourth of five children in a millworker's family. Only a generation removed from the farm, she came to dread those visits to the country, the family homesteads where her grandparents raised cattle and hogs and vegetables to stock their cupboards in the winter. The rustic self-sufficiency was one thing, offering a measure of novelty and charm. But she never cared much for the back-breaking work that awaited in the fields, and even less for the late night visits made to the outhouse. She was barely ten when she vowed forever to be a "city-girl."

Looking back on her childhood days, when the seeds were planted for her time as a poet, Paul remembers being the "odd kid," full of doubts and misgivings, a feeling that something fundamental was wrong. Specifically, she brooded about the disconnect between professions of brotherhood and charity that she heard every Sunday at her church and the color-conscious realities of southern life. As she came of age in the 1960s, she saw the turmoil of the civil rights years and brooded sometimes about the reasons behind it.

"I always wanted to know why," she says. "Why did we treat people differently because of the color their skin? I was always told, 'That's just the way it is.'"

Many years later, as a graduate student in 2008, she came across a book called *Killers of the Dream*, an extended essay by Lillian Smith, one of the great iconoclasts of southern letters. Writing in 1949, Smith set out to explain, intuitively from her first-hand encounters, the spirit-killing power of southern segregation. Smith, it should be noted, was white, a Georgian who came from a family of means, and when her book appeared in the 1940s it was received with horror in many parts of the South. Smith was one of the first to argue – with a power and eloquence that set her apart –that segregation was the natural heir to slavery, as crippling to whites as it was to the blacks it was meant to oppress.

"From the day I was born," Smith wrote, "I began to learn my lessons. I was put in a rigid frame too intricate, too twisting to describe here so briefly, but I learned to conform to its slide-rule measurements. I learned it is possible to be a Christian and a white Southerner simultaneously; to be a gentlewoman and an arrogant callous creature in the same moment; to pray at night and ride a Jim Crow car the next morning and to feel comfortable in doing both. I learned to believe in freedom, to glow when the word *democracy* was used, and to practice slavery from morning to night. I learned it the way all of my southern people learn it: by closing door after door until one's mind and heart and conscience are blocked off from each other and from reality."

Almost from the day she read those words, P.T. found herself in a flood of reflection – partly, at first, a rush of recognition about the habits of thought on which she was raised. It seemed, indeed, that Southerners had a deadly and unique gift for believing in contradictory things, for segregating their feelings and minds, and doing grave damage to their psyches in the process.

More seriously and consciously than ever before, Paul began to write about such things, to search through her poetry for her own understandings of what it meant to her to be a Southerner. She found bits and pieces of beauty in the search – in the southern landscape, in the food we eat and the ties that hold our families together despite the inevitable pain we inflict. She even found a dreadful beauty in the weather, in the summer heat and the hurricanes roaring in from the Gulf, and she writes about all these things in her poems. But there is more. She also writes about southern history and the life of her family, and the rural origins she found so problematic as a child.

Interspersed with the poems are essays adding depth to a narrative about southern life – one writer's deeply personal account, blending skillfully her own recollections with perspectives gained from other southern writers. The result is a thoughtful body of work, soaring in places, earthy in others, touching the heart and soul of the South.

– Frye Gaillard
Writer in Residence
University of South Alabama

TABLE OF CONTENTS

FOCUS ONE: *A Southerner Remembers*

FOCUS TWO: *The South – What Came Before*

FOCUS THREE: *A Southerner in the Twenty-First Century*

FOCUS FOUR: *The Living, Breathing South*

REFERENCES

Focus One

*A southerner remembers places,
people and events.*

*"The individual is an embodiment of external circumstances,
so that a personal story is a social story."*
"The Legacy of the Civil War," **Robert Penn Warren (1961)**

The Lesson Of Tides

If you ask me where I am from, there is no easy answer.

My home is in the ghostly corridors of Fort Morgan, where the blood of unknown soldiers stains the cold stones, and the bones of history lie scattered about like the dust of musket balls. My home hides among the knobby branches of two-hundred-year-old oaks in Cadillac Square, where the French signed one of their meaningless pieces of paper with the natives, thinking they were purchasing the island they named for their beloved Dauphin. It is in the deathless notes of the Excelsior Band as they wind their way from Joe Cain's resting place, stating and restating that when the Saints go marching in, they want to be in that number. It is in the advancing tide that uncovers pastel butterfly shells, but never reveals where their previous owners have gone. It is in the chambers of the sand dollar, where five bone-white doves hide, waiting for the clumsy to set them free.

Those who grew up with hurricanes understand what I am saying – that the name of home cannot be trusted to anything born of man and mortar.

When I was just five years old, listening to the rising tide of wind outside the window, I refused to pray *"if I should die before I wake, I pray, Dear Lord, my soul to take."* It was a little simple magic, but I hoped that God might spare our house if He thought He needed to work on my soul a little bit longer. Once, I thought it actually worked, that the storm had passed us by, until I opened the front door and discovered that our house was an island.

Our street had become a dirty river bearing red ant mounds like floating volcanoes, their occupants erupting and retreating over and over, their world tilting and turning in the wake of passing cars. Water moccasins curled on welcome mats and alligators prowled subdivisions, the boundaries of their territories lost in the rising waters. Feral dogs and cats defended stalled cars as their own, having been driven back to the realm of domesticity from the wildness they had chosen. They growled and hissed and spat from their small metal fiefdoms, railing even at would-be rescuers in their terror. All creatures are made equal by hurricanes; all storm-shocked, all exposed, all fearful. In the aftermath of a category five hurricane, home is whatever calms the heart; a dry, sheltered place, a cool drink, a warm meal, a familiar face, a pair of welcoming arms.

Anyone who grows up on the Gulf Coast learns these lessons of tides; the ways of wind and water, but they also learn the deeper meaning of stillness – as a harbinger of hurricanes, or as the precursor of a phenomenon indigenous to only a handful of places on earth.

When the tide goes flat, and the water becomes still, that is the first sign. In the full dark of a moonless night, my siblings could not see beyond the circles of their flashlights, did not notice that the waters they waded, gigging poles in hand, croaker sacks slung over their shoulders, had become still.

Stillness is an indication of saltwater stratification that occurs when fresh water flowing down from southwest Alabama rivers does not mix with the salt water of the Gulf of Mexico, but instead, lays on top of it like a plastic tarp, causing the salt water to become stagnant.

Of course, I did not notice because I was not allowed past the ruffled skirts of the tide line. I was only seven years old, and my siblings feared that I might step on a stingray. At least, that's what they said.

Stagnant water becomes deoxygenated, suffocating the microscopic creatures that live in the upper layer of the water, and causing them to sink to the bottom. Bacteria feed on the dead and dying, which further depletes the oxygen.

I remember kicking at the foam that edged the tide, sulking because I wasn't even trusted with a flashlight, but had to stand in the corona of a lone bulb hanging from the remains of a weather-eaten pier. My siblings yelled to each other, asking if anyone had spotted a flounder, or even a crab.

It was so subtle, I'm sure none of us noticed the second sign: a gentle wind blowing from the east, coupled with a rising tide. This wind pushes the upper layer of oxygen-laden water away from shore, as the rising tide pushes the deoxygenated water toward the coast.

The first thing I noticed was a crab limping slowly across my foot.

Considering the uncounted number of chicken necks I had lost in the bay in my quest to catch these creatures, the sight of a crab ignoring me was almost insulting. I glared at the creature as it traversed my tennis shoe.

I bent over to pick it up – so far, the only catch of the night.

That's when I noticed the others.

About two, or three, or four, dozen others.

Lacking any context with which to put this situation into perspective, I stood frozen in place, apparently captured by these creatures I had hunted all my short life.

I don't remember who yelled "JUBILEE!"

I just remember bolting for the car.

That night, the bay became an abattoir, as my siblings scooped up gasping aquatic creatures with their nets or their bare hands – bait buckets and ice chests and garbage bags and croaker sacks full. Only later, bellies and freezers packed, could we appreciate what a fragile phenomenon we had witnessed. If even one of those circumstances had changed – the direction of the wind, or the sequence of the tide – that jubilee, and our subsequent jubilation, would never have occurred.

Perhaps my love for the cold, silent corridors of Fort Morgan is an acceptance, an embracing, of these lessons I have learned. Soldiers built the stone and brick edifice of the fort with the ballast from their ships, thinking that this outpost on the tip of the island that guarded the entrance to Mobile Bay would enable them to protect their harbor from invaders. Standing on the prow of this abandoned fortress, I scan the waters where luckless ships, bearing fortunes and futures, went down. Beneath these waves men breathed their last in an iron-clad coffin while Admiral Farragut *"damned the torpedoes"* and sailed *"full speed ahead"* into history. He and his men rest upon the bones of the French and Spanish invaders who claimed this spit of sand before them; an island created, and eternally recreated, by hurricanes.

Undoubtedly, the manic gaiety of Mardi Gras is an *"eat, drink and be merry"* response to this specter of destruction that hangs over Mobile like the Spanish Moss draping the ancient oaks that bow to each other over Government Boulevard. In fact, King Felix commands it when he arrives from the Isle of Joy to begin his annual misrule with the proclamation *"Laissez les bon temps rouler!"* From that moment on, until the bells toll in the atonement of Lent, the good times roll like a serpentine, zydeco tsunami. Even the wailing trek to the cemetery to mourn the passing of founder Joe Cain erupts into the "second line" that dances away from his grave, high stepping parasols leading the way – every movement, every voice, every hand waved in the air celebrating the fact that life goes on.

Fantastic floats that wobble their way around Bienville Square on Mardi Gras Day; papier-mâché and chicken wire schooners dedicated to myth and fairy tale, will die at Lent to be reborn in new themes before the next Easter. If I close my eyes, I can hear the crack of doubloons striking the plate glass windows of darkened shops, the rattle and clack of glass and plastic beads twirled above a waiting crowd, the clop of horses and the rhythmic strains of marching bands testifying, and, above all, the anonymous, eternal, ever-new voice of a child yelling, *"Hey, Mister, throw me something!"* These sights and sounds are no less transient than the high and low tides of human desire, no less permanent than hope and joy.

When I was very young, I marveled over each shell I found on the white sands of Gulf Shores, wondering how the former occupant could cast away such a beautiful home. When I was older, there was a sigh of understanding when I read that the shells I found were simply temporary shelter for creatures whose lives could be lost in finding or creating their next abode. Indeed, my treasured multicolored butterfly shells, so loved because they resemble the wings of butterflies opened in flight – a visual paradox for the playful mind; hard "wings" like lacquered silk with mother-of-pearl linings – were cast aside so that the soft creature within could bury itself in the sand to begin its next incarnation. Where was the logic in creating a beautiful, disposable carapace for a short-lived creature incapable of appreciating that beauty? In time, my gaze shifted more and more from the treasure in my hand to the wave-polished sand where the previous owner had dived into mysteries into which I could not delve.

I realized that I was no more secure in our three-bedroom ranch-style bungalow in Whistler than was the boneless bivalve within his butterfly-wing shell. I had learned the lesson of tides – that only the flexible, the malleable, the soft survive – the hard are cast aside, broken down and recycled.

Like a crab, I carry a hard shell of experience, but I discard my preconceived ideas when they prevent me from learning and adapting. Like Fort Morgan, I am built of the cold stones of logic – of the wars that rage within me, only ghosts remain in the end. Like the unseen previous owner of the butterfly shell, I accept that life is a trade-off – the old for the new.

I carry within me, fresh and vibrant, the jubilant sounds of the Excelsior Band, that long-ago sight of my first butterfly shell, the musty silent smell of the cool corridors of Fort Morgan, the exquisite starched-doily texture of a fragile sand dollar cradled in my palm, and the liquid susurrations of the tides of the Gulf of Mexico – the continual "shushing" of mother ocean.

If you ask me where I am from, this is my answer.

Cold Fried Chicken In Cadillac Square
(Dauphin Island, Alabama, Summer circa 1960)

We always roll our Chevy into Cadillac Square
like faithful citizens of France
come to reclaim this part of the island for their beloved Dauphin.

Past the rusted anchor chain, hard right and creak to a stop,
lawn chairs sprung on loamy sand with a "plop".

Mama and Daddy homestead with R.O.C. Cola,
a well-thumbed copy of *"Gone With the Wind,"*
a radiating basket of cooling fried chicken
and a small black A.M. radio tuned to Red Sox or Grand Ole Opry-
                    whichever comes in clearest.

Kids in Keds ascend bearded grandfather oaks
like Autumn reversed, in high gear,
with whoops and dares and Tarzan yells
from Johnny Weismuller "wannabe's"
and raspberries from Cheeta critics. *(And everyone's a critic.)*

Future second-string quarterbacks chuck apple cores like pros,
while future prom queens skin their noses.
(Unfortunately, future nurses are not yet
a twinkle in Daddy's eye, so best not to cry.)

It don't take no government agency to tell you
that Spanish Moss makes treacherous Tarzan vines.
(This is the age of common sense;
just a peachfuzz shadow past the age of innocence.)

"Bless this food, Oh Lord, to the nourishment of our bodies
and our souls to Thy service. Amen." (Lord, let us begin.)

Sinners of the highest order we aspire to be, (secretly)
as Gluttony and Sloth cast chicken bones for our souls
on the leaf-and-acorn crabboil poured out by last night's rain.

(Wishes are split between locked pinkies, lost on a pull of the wrist,
then stashed in creaking gloveboxes
to be forgotten like pecking orders when tummies are tight
and all the best pieces are gone, anyway.)

Day bungles forward on the backs of single-minded black ants
plundering bits of knuckle and skin from underneath our dangling feet,
navigating femurs and backbones with the same determination we show
to the intoxicating wine of twilight – they stumble out of reach
just as we stumble toward the back seat.

"Go round, go round, little Alice Blue Gown,
we'll all be together about sundown…"*
(Daddy always mumbles songs that seem appropriate at the time,
but only songs that rhyme.)

Rumbling back to the suburbs of Whistler,
piled up with tangled curls and dirty feet,
while Little Jimmy Dickens on the radio allows
as how at Sunday dinner little kids like us might just as well
"take an old, cold tater and wait.."**,
we cannot know that time has just left on our plates
a memory more satisfying than cold fried chicken.

* "Little Alice Blue Gown / Cajon Love Song" - traditional
** "Take an Old Cold Tater (And Wait)" - Bartlett, by Little Jimmy Dickens

Dreams Of Revelations

When I was a child, hurricanes came in boxes;
small, black, plastic boxes
with shiny, round eyes
and teeth
that wouldn't pick up any stations,

but grinned like a Cheshire Cat
all the while
that Daddy fiddled with the dials –

even hisssssssssing its refusal
to spit out
locations,
coordinances,
latitudes –

an attitude *allowed*
from small, black, plastic boxes –

while short, white, lumpy candles
stood at the ready,
their wicks practically lusting
for the tongues
of sharply-struck kitchen matches –

all the night sullen,
"swole-up" with desire for rain,

damn the cost
in children lost
on their knees
or on their backs.

The ticking of the wind-up clock
soaked the ticking of our beds.

Dreams of Revelations
festered in our heads.

And I refused
to pray.

9

Truth Be Told

When I was seven, Mama took the belt to me
because I wished that I was
black –

beat me till my skin screamed
white-whiskered scarlet welts,
but, I wouldn't take it back.

Black
was blue fire, sorghum voiced Bird of Paradise Jubilation Angels
calling down the Rapture.

Black
was hot-pink, silk-wrapped, writhing slain-in-the-spirit honey rivers
flowing to the Judgement Seat.

Black
was joyous-tear-stained, lace-edged,white handkerchief doves
flying in the face of Satan,
flapping to make him lose all patience
with sinners like me.

Black

was what I wanted to be

while Mama's belt cracked behind me
like Papa Lee's bullwhip raining fire and brimstone on a wandering steer –
and, suddenly, it was all so clear;

Mama LIED to me
when she told me
I could be

ANYTHING

I wanted to be.

Indian Love Song
(For Joe Cain, wherever he may be.)

I knew it would never work,
given the fact that I was seven
and he was dead,

but I wanted to marry him,
anyway,
at least one day a year.

It was unrequited, of course,
he would never notice me
among all the weeping widows
who shuffled to his grave.

But, I was better than them –
I "got" him –
in his buckskins and eagle feathers,
we had something important in common.

In neighborhood skirmishes
I CHOSE to be the Indian,
whooping my way through azalea can-
yons,
snatching off cowboy hats
to grab buzzcuts by the handful.

My rubber knife pressed to sweaty fore-
heads
I demanded "SAY it!"
until they grumbled "you win."

My Indian name
was MRS. Slacabormorinico

and I, too,
was NEVER defeated
in battle.

Temptation, Tripe and Temperance

At the age of seven, I vowed that I would never again eat tripe

or plunge my August face into scalding cold artesian springs
vased in red pottery cisterns gurgling uncivilized
at the end of my grandfather's garden.

I would not swallow any beverage that came to me belly-warm
in silver pails from the lowing barn,
or eat produce gritty and still throbbing from the vine.

I was defining myself, and I had nothing to do
with mules turning sugarcane presses
to draw down red sorghum suns.

I was not the startled bream flashing counterfeit currency and coin
(his emerald, silver and gold distractions)
like a sideshow hawker
intent on picking your pocket of his freedom.

I was a city girl in Mary Janes and Dotted Swiss,
perched on a soda fountain stool
with my frosty mug of A&W Root Beer
and my hot pecan twist

and I would never again run colt-footed and bronze-chested
through a milkweed meadow wrapped in a butterfly cloud –

or, at least, I would never again eat tripe.

Daddy's People

If there ever was Eden, it is here
where the roads run off of any map and wild eyes stare
                    without fear.

There are creatures here that have never seen man
and will never be seen again.

My father has brought me to meet his people
before they die away.
                    I am ten.

I have been to the country, I think,
then the ruts become the road
and branches break on our rear-view mirrors.

We stop for a drink, wade through high aromatic grasses
and low scrub, grab the fluted edges of the ceramic pipe
and lean forward to plunge our faces into invisible cold.

Currents weave in the sand below, where water
                    abandons earth,
          scrolls like Sanskrit and erases itself.

Handshakes all around. Sandpaper hands
               that squeeze and release.
Leather hands with knobby knuckles and crescents of hard skin,
like countries of unknown terrain.

Skin stretched over sinew. Soil rubbed in like a birthmark.
Skin with splinters from the planks we stand on.
From the table we sit at. From the roof overhead.

Hands that pushed the plow offer me the greens.
Hands stained from shelling pass me the butter beans.
Hands that pulled the teats pour me milk that swirls
                    like white liquid marble
          in my chipped blue enamel cup.

I look up from my plate that holds this universe of earth,
know that I am unworthy,
                    and that I am forgiven.

13

Dangerous Places You Always Meant To Go

It isn't really fear you feel when your
    toes scrape bottom
        and you never meant to go there.

          Spasming some semblance of a dogpaddle,
      you think, oddly, to yourself, "People
   are supposed to float."

Where is that weightlessness
    that made people fear you were
        "just gonna blow away on a stiff breeze"?

          What good is having been accused of
             "bubbleheadedness" when your own breath
      bubbles effortlessly airward without you?

     Trapped in a transparent prison that
prisms prettily about you, you seem to have eternity
    to think of all the places you were not supposed to go:

         like "The Hangout" on a Friday night
            when packs of testosterone- fueled sportscars
              prowled the parking lot
            and "Freshman" was the flavor of the day,

          or the boys bathroom when raucous laughter
        curled in blue tendrils
      from underneath the door,

or "The Coed" when the Mardi Gras regatta
    was in port and the sailors were
        chalking their cues.

        But your parents never warned you
          about the bottom of Prichard Park Pool
          on a brillant August day
            when the lifeguard is busy twirling
         his shiny new whistle
      for the Whistler Girls' Softball Team.

Five-Day Backup Shift Change Hangover

Stale dust,
like the sterile sweat of despair,

coats the winding machine,
the cutter,
the box sealer,
the conveyor belt,
the stool,
your clothes,
your shoes,
your face.

Shadow-bearded workers,
their lips tinted black
by nicotine and caffeine,
mock your accent,
walk behind you,
their hands outstretched,
squeezing fistfuls of air
inches from your butt,
every time you cross the room.

Pretend
not to notice.

Is it worth this?

Working twelve-hour shifts
in cavernous rooms
made claustrophobic
by winding machine whines
and cutter confetti.

Confusing sunrise
with sunset.

Wondering if this
is the last night of graveyard shift
or the first overtime of three to eleven.

Worrying about
walking into the cutter blades
on a five-day backup shift change hangover.

Is it?

 Worth this?

Popping antihistamines to breathe,
aspirin to think,
vitamins to stay alive,
coffee to drive home.
Spending your fifteen-minute break slumped on your stool
with your head on the stopped conveyor belt
because it takes less energy than walking
to the break room.

 Is it?

Dragging yourself toward the sunrise/sunset,
craving bacon
and eggs
and ice cream
and quiet
and sleep,
trying to remember
where you left your innocence
and where you parked the car.

Ask yourself, again,
"Is a college education
really worth this?"

Pass your father
in the parking lot.

Remember

to smile.

Overflight

We built a fire on the beach,
fired up our brains
with cannabis and Boones Farm.

We were made harmless by night,
by the overflight of the Perseids,
by the clucking of the ocean's tongue.

We thought we were one with the universe,
sparks from our fire rising higher
than our imaginations could span.

We ran from an owl angered by the fire.
Our desire to fly, like sparks, expired.
Prostrate, we hid our eyes from the sky.

In His Father's House

My father hum-mumbles hymns –
his voice a slump-shouldered dog in the doorway,
  unsure of its welcome.

He reads Psalms 23 softly,
but with self-confidence.
  (He knows all the words by heart.)

We lose him on the Doxology, though,
as if the name intimidates him
  and his insecurity clenches his throat.

I want to tell him,
"God is not the father who told you,
  'books are no use loading a log skidder.'"

But, I don't.

Blessed are those
who have never known mercy
  and yet still believe.

Or What's A Heaven For?

Ah, but a man's reach should exceed his grasp,
Or what's a heaven for?
Robert Browning, "Andrea del Sarto"

My father longed to find the jar of coins
his father buried behind the house –
      coins that shamed him by making themselves
      precious in his eyes.

This memory, kudzu covered,
belonged to no man's map,
      but burned holes in his dreams
      and fell into the substratum of myth.

For my mother, it was her mother's bread bowl,
a hollowed, hallowed, wooden artifact
      that held her memories of winter mornings
      kneaded, knuckle-flattened, and lard risen.

Such a heart-breaking desire to face,
such a work-a-day heirloom to covet,
      when households lose the treasure of a parent's love
      and grown children become beggars in their own eyes.

Which was the greater tragedy? – a jar of coins lost
to the developers bulldozer, irredeemable under macadam,
      or a wooden bowl left on the porch in the freezing rain,
      thawing on a sun-split spring morning, breaking its only promise?

Earthiness

She was humus and decay, seven-day-old cow manure working alive
with grubs, fat black ants, and slimy tan earthworms –
                    manna for hydrangea.

She was mercuric earth nectar, stout as the buckets she drew it in,
tooth-chilling Chardonnay from God's own cellar –
sacrificial wine for gardenias
                    and American Beauties.

In the sepia photographs she hides her hands behind her back
to conceal her fingernails – nails brown and nibbled at the edges
like the photographs,
                    themselves.

The words that I remember grated on my ears –
dire warnings and admonitions that wriggled their way into my subconscious,
to lay dreams that hatched on suffocating nights
when thunder knocked the sawhorses
                    from underneath the washtub of the sky.

          I never saw her cry.

She died when I was grown and far from home,
bringing me back to a house that held her castoff memories
the way a Woolworths' plastic cemetery spray captures the body,
but never the soul,
                    of the flowers it portrays.

I am nothing like her – cannot bear even sterile city dirt beneath my fingernails,
and have been known to starve air plants with my horticultural disinterest –
but, in my mirror, blue/green/gray hydrangeas blossom
                    from the humus of my pupils.

Beauty Queens

Scooped up unprepared, nonetheless,
Big Mama's pets twirled like beauty queens
in an aerial promenade;
preening, spinning,
wingtips sometimes touching,
sometimes not.

Wind-choreographed flames
splashed against a sodden sky.

They dropped in reverse order,
as is the tradition, last to first,
molted from the stress of competition,
stripped of all delusions,
pale, dimpled candles blown out.

Losers – speechless – denuded,
shamelessly flung themselves
in dejection
over farmhouses,
outhouses, feedlots.

Startled farmers watched contestants rain down,
poked inconsolable fourth, third, second runners-up,
plucked their crimson feathers
out of rain barrels, asked,
"could these be Mrs. Lena's? Could they?"

The winner landed on a hay roll miles away,
held court over an empty field,
her head bowed in humility.

Of all my grandmother's mail-order
Rhode Island Reds,
her favorite – Miss Scarlet –
that tornado riding beauty queen
even made the front page
of the county farm agent's newsletter.

Old Time Religion

Wadn't nothing soft about her;
not her organ bench, not her playing,
no sotto voce in her psalms,
no fat on her bones.

"The Devil loves softness,
*   the Devil loves sloth."*

Stomp those organ pedals, slap those keys,
let them hear you at Calvary!
She sings, "Gimme that ol' time religion,
gimme that ol' time religion!"

"The Devil loves whispers,
*   the Devil loves lies."*

Yank those stoppers out, slam them flat –
the Devil is afraid of conviction like that!
"Gimme that ol' time religion –
it's good enough for me!"

"If you are neither hot, nor cold,
*   the Lord will spit you out!"*

The Devil loves lukewarm Christians,
he slurps them up like soup!
"Gimme that ol' time religion,
gimme that ol' time religion!"

Ain't no room for sentiment,
ain't no room for pity.
Life is hard, AMEN to that!
Yank those stoppers out, slam them flat!

"Gimme that ol' time religion-
it's good enough for me!"

Readin', Rightin' & 'Rithmatic

We lied – said that I
lived with my aunt
in Alabama Village.

I lived in fear of discovery.

Since I was not where
I professed to be,
no bus would come for me.

But, that was the point, you see –

to avoid that federally mandated ride
to the high school where I
had no legacy.

And from which came the opposite me.

In Civics class, we never read
how many individual rights it takes
to redeem a national inequity –

I just knew that I was no longer free.

Picklin' Time

alum and vinegar
    gossip and picklin' spices.
mulling over which jars for family,
    which for friends.
steam making mudpies
    of our makeup.

a rowdy cloud of bottleflies
    holding revival
in the peelings pan
    outside the back door.

"The Devil made you drop that jar,
    just to hear you fuss!"

capturing summer with a grunt
    and a hand-towelled
twist of the wrist.
    marking bold on the lid
as if any of it will last
    long enough to go bad.

how sad –
      we can save
    bread-and-butters –

      but not each other.

P.T. PAUL

That Last Furrow

My aunt squatted in her garden in Alabama Village
and shoved her cracked cuticles between the string beans
to pluck weeds before they could get a roothold
while death, unnoticed, reached inside her and plucked.

> Mobile to New Orleans in the moonlight –
> Picayunes and Jack Daniels, Waylon Jennings on the radio –
> he called himself "The Owl" or "The Ghost"
> and spoke to no one for days.

Her muscles, sprung from contractions, could not hold
her belly – a false pregnancy, it cast its own shadow.
Her toes splayed around black clods,
her heels were cracked as a dead riverbed.

> He introduced me to raw oysters in the front yard,
> sitting on an upsidedown bucket,
> red metal ice chest on one side, Mr. Jack on the other.
> *Someone* had to pave the driveway.

Women in my family have never cried for foolishness,
have never mourned the unborn children they lost –
gone to Jesus, praise the Lord, His Will be done –
this was the cost of womanhood; some blood and tissue,
the issue of humanity – there were always other mouths to feed.

> He wasn't a Coonass, but he patois'd like one,
> drank his coffee with chicory, smoked his Picayunes
> and ate beignets at midnight while the moon slid over Mobile Bay.

She had three in the ground, already – one lost before breath,
two to death before they knew their own names –
loss is all the same when you break it down to flesh and bones.

> He would flap that limp pinky of the shuckin' glove at me,
> *"dat dere's a warnin' fo' you, Cher,"*
> but, no bones lay among the crushed shells in the driveway.
> We stole the red ball from the smashed cab
> and put it in his rusty truck. We couldn't get the mudflaps.

She was not alone in this plucking – my aunt – and one day would recall
this moment in the bean patch to all her sisters
over coffee and iced tea on the front porch
while they plucked weeds of unhappiness from their childhood memories.

They put something on his stone about the war –
he would have liked that –
but he would have liked his red steering ball better,
clutched in that oyster-shucking gloved right hand,
with Mr. Jack by his side for company.
He might even have laughed if he'd seen her in the parking lot,
leading the Second Line, hem of her dress flipping around,
hands waving insolent in the magnolia'd breeze –
he might have said, *"dance, Cher – I don' blame you."*

She fed eight children from that garden in Alabama Village,
raised pecks of string beans, bushels of okra, gallons of cucumbers,
a melon or two, but mostly tomatoes – Beefeaters big as a grown man's fist,
vinebreakers more tart than sweet,
more claret than scarlet,
firm, smooth skinned
and thick-juiced on your tongue.

Another Tower, Another War

I would keep the memory of the climb to the top of the fire tower; the jangling steel steps that drained the marrow from my leg bones, the trembling railing that channeled the force of the switching winds, the view from the top that froze me in place and left me staring over the cliff to where the mountain fell away three times as far down as I had climbed up. I would keep that dry-eyed recognition that below me lay Big Creek Lake in west Mobile County, sometimes called Converse Reservoir, where he had taken me to fish miles from family and friends, where he laughed at me when I ran from the rattlesnake, where I first learned that fear is the father of courage, and that my first impulse was to run, not fight. I would keep the righteous anger that lifted my feet and sent me stomping down the stairs when he teasingly threatened to leave me on that platform, then turned himself and ran, screaming down the stairs like a banshee with a death wish, high on youth, testosterone, pot and Budweiser. I would keep the insight that made me refuse to take his hand at the bottom of the tower – a gesture he seemed to think excused any deed – and the resolve to never see him again that made me slam the car door when he opened it for me. But, I would lose the innocence and optimism that made me forgive him when he turned my face toward him and pressed his nicotine flavored lips to mine. And I would take back my answer when he looked into my eyes, told me the eternal lovers' lie, and asked me to trust him forever.

Down Alabama Highway 112, between Bay Minette, Alabama and Cantonment, Florida, standing like the gnomon of a sundial in the baked Baldwin County landscape, is a rusted fire tower. Its shadow has marked the growing up and cutting down of generation after generation of loblolly pine forests owned by Kimberly-Clark Paper Company, forests that hem in the farm where my mother grew up. In the manic first years of America's involvement in World War II, my mother climbed that tower and recorded the passing of every airplane that traversed this airspace, her ritual a prayer for the safe passage of my father, her fiancé, through the European Theatre "Fire and Ice Campaign" of General Patton. While she scoured familiar skies, my Dad slogged his jeep through stripped French vineyards, got his supply truck lost behind enemy lines in Germany, and hid the generals' staff car in the barn of a sympathetic farmer in Sicily while the enemy double-marched in retreat through the ruined fields that surrounded him. His only comfort sometimes lay in the knowledge that those back home were safe from the enemy he fought, and his dream was that his wartime journey would end back where it began, in the front yard of his parents house, with his family surrounding him and his arms around my mother. This was what kept him focused in those foreign, treacherous lands. This was his truth. This was his prayer.

Back in Baldwin County, Alabama, an hour north of the Gulf of Mexico, my mother carried to the fire tower a chart of military aircraft, their silhouettes and signage, their crew requirements and cargo capacities. She compared every plane she spotted to German Arados, Heinkels and Messerschmitts, pored over drawings of Greif long-range bombers and Junkers bomber/reconnaissance planes, wondered if the hum of a crop-duster was actually the drone of a Siebel Si 201 STOL reconnaissance aircraft, worried that her untrained eyes might miss the silhouette that could carry the war to her own front yard – not knowing that it was already in her back yard. How soundly would she have slept, had she known that in May and June of 1942, the Gulf of Mexico was the most dangerous place in the world for shipping, as some fifty freighters and tankers were sunk by German U-boats in the sea-lanes between Florida and Texas? Residents of the coast wondered at the explosions and the glowing lights on the horizon, not realizing that these were the funeral pyres of American ships sunk within domestic waters, or that about two dozen German submarines prowled their own white sand shores.

During the week, my mother packed boxes in the munitions factory in Pensacola, Florida, gossiping with her sisters and cousins about the love affairs that flourished or withered during the long months between letters. After her shift, she climbed the metal stairs of the fire tower, her notebook and binoculars in hand, her mind simultaneously on the past and the future, a black and white photo of my father in her pocket. The melody of a popular song *"When the Lights Go On Again All Over the World"* played out in her head and she sang along,

> *"When the lights go on again all over the world,*
> *And the ships will sail again all over the world,*
> *Then we'll have time for things like wedding rings*
> *and free hearts will sing,*
> *When the lights go on again all over the world."*

She stood on the wooden planking that covered the observation deck, listening for the hum of an approaching airplane, wondering if the ordnance she had packed would find its way to my father, if it would arrive too late to save him, or if it would be waylaid and used against him. They had made a promise to each other, my parents-to-be, that they would maintain a stubborn optimism no matter what, in spite of what the newspaper might say, and in defiance of the naysayers who would have every battle lost, they would remain resolute in their belief that the war, and their story, would have a happy ending. They were young. They could believe in such things.

"It is certain that all on board perished," was the report of Captain H.E. Shonland, of the U.S.S. San Francisco, responding to the sinking of the U.S.S. Juneau on the moonless evening of November 12th, 1942, at Guadalcanal. That report was classified, and the Navy kept the information confidential so that the enemy would not know the extent of the damage inflicted during the thirty minutes of close combat in which five U.S. ships were lost.

When their call to arms came, my father, his brothers, and his cousins trooped down to the recruiting office together and enlisted at the same time, hoping to serve in the same company, but their request was denied with no explanation. Only later would they, and the rest of the world, be informed that all five sons of Tom and Alleta Sullivan of Waterloo, Iowa, perished in the sinking of the U.S.S. Juneau.

Tom and Alleta Sullivan simply stopped receiving letters from their boys – George, Francis, Joseph, Madison and Albert – then they received a letter of condolence from President Franklin Roosevelt. Pope Pius XII sent his personal letter of regret, along with a silver religious metal and a rosary.

Alleta Sullivan removed her star flag from the front window, replaced the five blue stars with gold ones and sewed a black border around it.

Her remaining child, Genevive, joined the WAVES in June of 1943, and Alleta christened a new destroyer, *"U.S.S. The Sullivans,"* in San Francisco.

After the war, Gunner's Mate Allen Heyn, one of several survivors of the Juneau, would reveal that among those men not killed during that tragic battle was George Sullivan. For ten days, the survivors waited for rescue, enduring intense heat, festering wounds, and the constant circling

29

of sharks. One night, delirious from hunger and thirst, George Sullivan decided to take a bath, took off his clothes, and slipped into the water.

Heyn would later say, simply, *"That was the last I saw of him."*

The *"Fighting Sullivan Brothers"* became the symbol of ultimate sacrifice among the American population – who could refuse to offer less to their country? My father, his brothers, and his cousins departed separately, in silence, hugging their families for a long time in the front yard of my grandparents' house in Gateswood, Alabama, too humbled by the national tragedy to question their separation, too proud to begrudge the country their support. My mother wondered only if she would be luckier than Alleta Sullivan, should my father be lost. Would she be spared the torture of not knowing? This was the anxiety that turned her feet to lead every time she walked to the mailbox – would there be a letter? And, if so, would it bear the hand-scrawled postage mark *"soldier mail?"*

Or would the return address be Washington, D.C.?

The walk from the porch to the mailbox became my mother's personal torture, but only for reasons that she already knew of, and her suffering, though great, was less for that. She walked in the trust of a young woman who thought that she knew her enemies, thought that she could name them, could face them, if necessary, could stare them down, and that made the climb up the fire tower her personal act of faith.

When the stock market crashed in 1929, ushering in the Great Depression, folks in Gateswood read the newspapers and shook their heads.

What was that far away financial disaster to men whose fortunes lay in mule-plowed fields germinating dreams of corn, potatoes, okra and beans? Surrounded by loblolly pine forests, my mother slept within a house handmade by my grandfather, on a mattress sewn and stuffed by my grandmother, and under quilts pieced by the Lady's Circle of Clear Springs Baptist Church, whose needles stitched the community lives together over log cabin patterned tops with feed sack backings. My father fell in love with her the first time he saw her, as a boy, when he helped his father deliver their hogs to my grandfather's farm where the hickory and pecan wood awaited the match in the smoke house, and my grandfather's pay was taken in ham and bacon.

When the war tore my parents apart, they pledged their lives to each other, to the dreams of future and family they had woven as children while picking blackberries in the hollow or floating the tangled branches of the Styx River in inner tubes, trailing fingers and laughter in that freezing stream. Their dream for me was actually a reprise of their own dream, their definition of *"happily ever after"* manifested in a three bedroom bungalow in Whistler, just north of Mobile, Alabama, where my father raised tomatoes in the flower beds among my mothers' roses – a constant source of embarrassment to me – but, an acknowledgement of the necessity of self-sufficiency and a reminder of the hunger that he carried with him through the ruined vineyards of France.

Their mantra was *"never again"* – never again to be separated by oceans or acts of congress, never again to fall asleep alone at night wondering if the stars would fall from the sky and incinerate their dreams, never again to fear the arrival of the postman or a soldier with a somber face, never again to be the frightened lovers whose hearts hung in the wind of war, twisting, tattered and torn. All my life, my parents warned me, *"You just wait until you have a husband... a house of your own... a family to raise"* because in their lexicon of experience there was only marriage, parenthood, grandparenthood. What else, in a world filled with death and destruction, would they have risked their lives for? What better legacy could they offer me?

"Whatta ya think, MoBEEL?" my boyfriend laughed, as he turned and charged down the steps, trailing a war whoop behind him, his flannel shirttail flapping in the wind, his boots glancing off the metal stairs as his hands slid down each offsetting railing.

I shook my head. I had long ago given up on the idea that I could correct his misnomer about my hometown, or that I even wanted to, since *"WHISTler"* sounded even more potentially annoying than *"MoBEEL."* Perhaps I was finally learning to pick my battles.

We had been dating for months, and yet he knew nothing of my parents' story, knew very little about me, except that I was a tomboy and a rebel, attributes he deduced from my behavior around him. In the short time he had known me, I had never turned the rear view mirror of the car so that I could see to put on lipstick or check my hair, like other girls my age. In fact, instead of running from the rain, I would lift my face to a sudden downpour and stand, oblivious to my surroundings, like a plant celebrating the end of a long dry spell.

He had watched me climb trees for a stolen view of outdoor concerts by Wet Willie and Lynyrd Skynyrd, had handed me a pistol with the intention of teaching me to shoot, then fallen silent to the *"plink"* of soda cans doing back-flips off a fence, had breathed a bemused *"daaaaamn"* when I took my first toke of pot and tried to blow a smoke ring. What he could not know was that I lay awake at night, not daring to dream of a life that did not include him, a life uncharted by anyone but myself, a life that wrote its own plot and denouement, that needed no editor but time and its secretary wisdom.

What he would never know was that his dream for us so closely resembled my parents' dream for me that I weighed his words of desire and devotion like coins in my hand, the price of cowardice, of self-betrayal, almost palpable, cold and hard. At this point, my heart hung between my ribs like a weathered plank on the deck of a fire tower.

From the top of my fire tower, I could see Big Creek Lake, part of a water system spawned by the influx of workers into the Port City during World War II, a beautiful necessity shimmering below me. From my left, winged a hawk tilting on the updraft, his white belly shining as he wheeled away, and I reached in my pocket for the notebook and pen I had left on my bed. To my right, roiled the noxious exhaust clouds of Scott Paper Company, those sulfuric fumes that my father insisted smelled *"like bacon and eggs."*

Twelve hours earlier, after a sixteen-hour shift, I had left that mill covered with sweat and paper dust, weary and bitter, depressed and exhausted. The words of my uncle, tossed at me before my shift as we passed in the parking lot, *"Your Daddy's real proud of you – he says you're a real worker!"* still rang in my ears.

My Dad's last words to me as I walked out the door to drive to work had been, *"If you leave this house before you are married, you can never come back."*

The scholarship letter from the University of Alabama lay in the bottom of my trashcan, next to last month's work schedule, spooned with my bank statement, nestled among glossy brochures of campuses with brownstones, bell towers and cobblestone streets.

As I followed my inebriated boyfriend down the steps and to the car, I thought about war, any war, every war, about how, even when it was unavoidable, it could destroy every tree and house and barn in its path, leaving entire countries liberated, shell-shocked, starving and naked. My parent's war had involved the entire world, and yet they had hoped and prayed and waited it out. My personal war had lasted my entire life, my only victory so far was half of a Bachelor's Degree, and lately, my parents and I had reached a stalemate of wills, an impasse of beliefs. The words "Pyrrhic Victory" floated through my head, the imagined voice of that ancient Roman General Pyrrhus stating, *"One more such victory and Pyrrhus is undone."*

The year was 1974, I was twenty-one, a junior at the University of South Alabama, and I was tired. He was a graduating senior, a boy from Birmingham, Alabama, who promised me the world, who gave me pot and beer, and who I thought I might actually love.

"Come on, MoBEEL," he crooned, as he wrapped his arms around me and leaned against the car. *"Whatta ya think?"* He pulled me close and pressed his nicotine-flavored lips to mine, and my protests died in my throat. He had the brown curls of a cherub, green eyes scattershot with topaz shards, and a five-o'clock shadow. When he wrapped his arms around me like night around the moon, my heart slowed, thought seemed unnecessary. In a moment, he released me, cupped my face in his hands, smiled his lopsided, stoned smile, and whispered the eternal lovers' lie: *"I just want to make you happy."* Once more, he stared into my eyes, his pupils dilating in the fading light, and whispered, *"Will you?"*

It seems like I held my breath forever.

Focus Two

The South
What Came Before

"...the notion of place has a natural relation to the notion of identity in community, in the shared place."
"The Legacy of the Civil War," **Robert Penn Warren (1961)**

It Is Written
(A Found Poem)

There are theories, including the piezoelectric effect
(voltage created by squeezing rock), as well as exoelectron emissions,
(reminiscent of phosphorescence), even sonoluminescence, which is emitted
from imploding bubbles in a liquid *"excited by sound."*
But, it is written, *"And God said, Let there be light."*

When the cities of Helike and Bura in Greece were destroyed in 373 BC,
it was recorded that *"immense columns of flame"* preceded the destruction.
And in 1811, *"two vast electrical columns shot up from the eastern horizon"*
near the New Madrid Fault, one half-hour before sunrise,
as observed by a traveler on the Mississippi. We are also told,
"And the Lord went before them...by night in a pillar of fire, to give them light..."

In addition, it was reported in 1811 that the Mississippi River flowed backwards
"at the speed of a fast horse," that the Falls of Ohio dropped over 26 feet.
There was underground thunder, a *"tremendous upheaval"* felt 800 miles away,
vertical walls of water and a large hole in mid-river.
Firmin La Roche, French fur trader from St. Louis, wrote
"we believed we must surely die."

In the oil district of Petrolia, in Canada, in 1895,
a borehole struck a reservoir of gas
that ignited in a column of flame;
causing burning bitumen to fall in showers, *"like brimstone."*

It has been recorded that earthquakes around the Dead Sea
can cause an eruption of saline water
that forms a brine thick with mud,
encasing everything that does not move
in a mound or column or pillar of salt,
but none of this was written
before Lot led his family out of Sodom.

Afterward the account was written of their terrified flight
and the angel's warnings,
but not Edith's last word before her lips crusted over

and her mouth filled with brine,
which surely, when she turned back –
as any mother might do to check on her daughters –
could not have been anything more innocuous,
or damning, than *"hur…"*

The Pelican Girls
(A Found Poem)

In the Year of Our Lord, 1704,
By order of his majesty, the King, the following maidens shall be conveyed
to Fort Louis, in the colony of Mobile, on the good ship Pelican, to marry our Cana-
dian volunteers:

Jean Catherine de Berenhard

Francoise Marianne De Boirenard

Gabrielle Bonet

Marie Briard

They have come from orphanages and convents with letters of
recommendation, have won the "lottery," proved their virtue, passed
every test. They are allowed one suitcase.

Marie Thereze Bronchon

Genvieve Burel

Jeanne Burel

Marguierite Burel

His Majesty commends them to the care of the captain and crew of the good
ship Pelican and the keeping of Father La Vente that they will arrive in the
new land virgins, as their contract stipulates.

Catherine Christophe

Elizabeth Deshayes

Angelique Drouin

Marie Dufresne

They are tempted, sorely tempted, by the officers and crew, suffer
seasickness, are plagued by mosquitoes in Havana, bring unseen stowaways
back to the ship with them.

Renee Gilbert

Marguerite Guichard

Louise Margauerite Housseau

Louise Francois Le Fevre

One succumbs to the fever before reaching Dauphin Island, others bring it to their wedding beds. Les Femmes Cassettes bring the Yellow Death – and their little suitcases.

Marie Jeanne Marie

Marie Noel du Mesnil

Marie Madeline Ouanet

Marie Philipe

Most fulfill their contracts, some marry well, raise families, as the records reflect. Mobile is established, well and truly, for the Glory of France and her King.

Jeanne Elizabeth le Pinteux

Gabrielle Savarit

Marguerite Tavernier

Louise Francois Le Fevre dies on arrival of Yellow Fever. Gabrielle Bonet is deserted by her groom and, to this day, wanders the dunes of Dauphin Island in her petticoat with her long hair tangled in the wind, searching, watching, crying.

In the Year of Our Lord, 1704,
by order of his majesty, the King, twenty-three maidens were conveyed to Fort Louis, in the colony of Mobile, on the good ship Pelican, to marry Canadian volunteers for the glory of France.

La Femme Cassette

Is it your voice I hear on the parapet when the trade winds wail?
Are you waiting for your bridegroom to come home from the sea
as he promised on your wedding night, before the topsail swelled?
Is that you in the dunes, your pitch-black hair flying free?

You arrived with your prayer book, *La Femme Cassette,*
with the blessings of the King, your destiny in hand,
left *The Pelican* and your chaperones with no regrets,
set foot on Dauphin Island, your own Promised Land.

Was it only your innocence that he took, Orphan Child,
and did you curse him with fever? Did he languish, alone?
Did he call out your name, as your own heart went wild?
Does it matter, in the end, when all hope is gone?

Do you wander, in your petticoat, when the trade winds wail?
Is that your voice I hear on the parapets, sweet Gabrielle?

Special Field Orders Number Fifteen
(A Found Poem)

*"If poetry is the little myth we make, history is the big myth we live,
and in our living, constantly remake."*
The Legacy of the Civil War," Robert Penn Warren

Mathew Brady never actually took all of the photographs attributed to him,
but claimed "The Dead of Antietam" that shocked the curious of New York, and
was not above posing fallen soldiers to make his point. He made his name, but
lost his fortune, chronicling the war.

Congress purchased the entire archive in 1875.

Thoreau, Emerson, and the Transcendentalists railed against industrialization,
cheered the Abolitionists, sanctified John Brown, but stood revealed after the War
when James Russell Lowell realized that the reformers were ready to reform
"everyone but themselves."

Emerson actually asked, *"Are they MY poor?"*

Preston Brooks drew the first blood of the Civil War on the floor of the Senate
when he caned Charles Sumner – the last was shed at the Battle of Blakeley
hours after the surrender of Lee at Appomattox. Between the caning and the
signing, 620,000 lives were lost –

more than in any American war before or since.

General Tecumseh Sherman's Special Field Order Number 15 promised forty
acres and a mule to any man of color who would fight for him. Even Lincoln
admitted the Emancipation Proclamation *"was of doubtful constitutional warrant."*
General Grant, two years before the war, *"had had to be locked howling drunk in a
steamboat cabin."*

The Constitution of the Confederacy forbade the slave trade.

Colonel Robert Gould Shaw, commander of the black Fifty-fourth Massachusetts,
was buried in a ditch under his own men in his first charge on Fort Wagner.
In 1870, Negroes finally won the right to vote. General Grant died of cancer,
discredited, broke, was carried to his final rest by Confederate Generals. General
Sherman's Special Field Order Number Fifteen was almost immediately counter-
manded by his commanding officer.

No one ever received forty acres and a mule.

White Sheets

The first time I saw the men in white sheets
they galloped across the silver screen
of the Saenger Theatre like summer thunder,
D.W. Griffith's quintessential boogiemen,
anonymous shoe tips peeping out from under seams,
the embodiment of a nation's racist dreams.

That was the summer of my own anxious dreams,
sleep-starved and sweating under white sheets,
my childhood coming apart at the seams
as I watched other children on a small silver screen
being beaten with batons by uniformed boogiemen –
blows crashed on their bodies like summer thunder.

Nitrogen is released by summer thunder
to waken the fields from their spring-fed dreams
while seeds slumber ignorant of insect boogiemen
and rain shatters down in crystal white sheets,
as children search the oracle of the silver screen,
knowing nothing it says is ever what it seems.

But, that is the nature of change, it seems,
that beliefs should be shot-gunned like summer thunder,
and a nation defined on a silver screen,
fed the hateful pabulum that sickens its dreams.
Fear and anger shaped the faces under those white sheets,
and ignorance is the anonymous, eternal boogieman.

There are those who steal the right to proclaim boogiemen,
to rend the fabric of society from seam to seam,
hiding their own agenda under white sheets
and roaring with the authority of summer thunder –
these are the villains who poison our dreams
and project their own hatred onto silver screens.

The first time I saw them on the silver screen,
was the last time I saw D.W.'s boogiemen
except in fever-tossed childish dreams,

while mountainous clouds, ripped apart at their seams,
gave birth to galloping summer thunder
that bore demons with eyeholes burning through white sheets.

Those white sheets still gallop across silver screens,
hollow as summer thunder, our eternal boogiemen,
the heritage, it seems, of a nation's racist dreams.

Photo Gravure

In 1862, they posed them just so;
        plump hands folded underneath rouged cheeks,
limp bodies coyly sprawled on satin pillows
        in the wanton innocence of childhood.

Stockings drooped as if they'd just collapsed from play –
        one unbuttoned shoe perhaps on the floor,
petticoats peeping impishly from rumpled skirts –
        no Botticelli cherub ever flirted so with light.

Sepia belies the telltale tint
        of Yellow Fever.
Photo Gravure creates shadows
        where Small Pox left its mark.

Matthew Brady snapped them all
        fallen riders of wooden steeds
and broken drummer boys
        in tattered dress grays, just alike.

No child, before or since
        ever held so still
for their first and last portrait,
        breathless for all eternity.

Progress

I'd like to think I could remember her name
the way I remember her "bird-in-the-treetop" laugh,
or the pearl of milk in the corner of her baby's smile,
or the way I pulled back my finger from touching his dimple.

We were in the birthing room of toilet tissue and pop-up Kleenex,
up to our ankles in the afterbirth of paper lint and heavy white dust.
And, above the exhausted metallic wheeze
of the winding machine winding down
before the "Bar-Ups" moved in with their vacuums to blow the mill down,
we were parting ways after working side by side for three months.

I'd like to say I could remember her name
the way I remember that our Daddies had worked side by side
all the winding days of our growing up,
had fished together on the Causeway,
sharing R.O.C. Colas and mullet,
had wandered the empty sidewalks of Prichard together
when the union stripped the economy bare every four years
to give the workers five cents more an hour,
like locusts of progress.

I like to pretend that I remember her name
like I pretend that I am proud of having worked at the mill,
like I pretend that I would do it all again,
like I pretended that I couldn't resist touching her baby's flawless skin
when, after all those years I had almost believed
that separate really was equal
and that, in the normal geometry of our existence,
parallel lives could never meet.

Moonpies and Madness and Saltwater Taffy

Quicksilver Folly,
chasing Death in dark circles,
marshals mayhem down sleeps' phantom streets.

Doubloons glitter downward,
cracking darkened shop windows –
they litter the ground at my feet.

Moonpies and madness and saltwater taffy
surge over my head
rhythmically.

Broken beads sting my palms.
Someone steps on my coat.
I grind a po-boy under my knee.

They wink from the curb
in the yellow torch light,
on the dark lips of memorys' maw

and I grovel, still grasping
for the currency of childhood:
cheap silver coins of Mardi Gras.

Breakfast With God

God had breakfast with us this morning.
He sat in important silence
and sopped his biscuit in gravy.

His over-easy eggs did not even dare stare at him.

He will drink his coffee while
he reads the newspaper.
My mother will tend to his coffee cup.
We will leave them to their godly business
and build mud forts and lob pinecones
until called.

He built this house from nothing,
made the blue Chevy appear
from sulfuric clouds that belch
from his smoke stacks –
they smell of bacon and eggs,
so hath he said.

We worship him in silence
when we return home from school
and his bedroom door is closed.

Yea, verily, even the sun does not rule him.

His is the litany of seven-day backup,
time and a half, overtime.
His laundry will be done
and his meals on the table
when he walks into the house,
his Grand Ole Opry on the radio,
or his Gunsmoke on tv,
so be it.

We sing hymns to him
when the car radio falls silent
and the road stretches dumbly before us.

Our journeys trace his Godly roots,
the red clay hills where he was formed,
arrows of gold-tufted corn
point us down the right path.

One long-ago summer
I looked up from the batter's box
and he was in the stands.
My hands trembled
and I swung on ignoble air,
ashamed that he was there to see it.

His is the transmutation of loblolly pines
to the paper on which our history will be writ,
and our family will be independent
and prosper for it.

Yes, God had breakfast with us this morning.

And he asked Himself to bless it.

Always, There Was the Heat

bearing down like the sweaty palm of poverty,
saying, *"NO – you will NOT rise up!"*
worse – in the night – a master bedded with a favored slave,
the moon grinning through the window,
winged roaches smacking into rusted screens.

Only pride can scour away the grime salt-crusted to tired skin.

Only hope would draw paper mill exhaust
into hitching, yellowed lungs
to drive the engine
that trundles over the moonscape of despair
everyday
to nowhere.

And, hope was always there,
a fever pumping Meadow Gardens Baptist Church paper fans
that boasted,

   "OUR God is a RIGHTEOUS God!"

while half-hearted *"AMEN"s*
and *"HALLELUJAH"s*
droned upward like bloated bluebottle flies
to tangle with the tacky blades
of a twirling ceiling crucifix
dedicated to some lesser god
who offered comfort in return for resignation –
a fair exchange, as the heat bears down.

FOCUS THREE

A Southerner
In the Twenty-First Century

"We Southerners are a mythological people
created half out of dream and half out of slander."
Jonathan Daniels, former Raleigh newspaper editor
Pop Culture, Y'all come: Exhibit Focuses on Southern Stereotypes
Leigh Dyer, McClatchy Newspapers, Sept., 20, 2007

Time Out of Mind

"Don't touch that radio!"

"I'm sorry, Mr. Paul, I was just gonna turn it up a little. How's that?"

"That's just right. I always did like Little Jimmy Dickens. Don't you?"

"Sure, Mr. Paul, me too. What's the name of that song, again?"

He bumps along, his hands at ten and two o'clock, humming his out of tune mumble-hum. We are going to Philadelphia, Mississippi, to my Uncle Ted's farm, and it's all lumpy back roads, kudzu canyons and suspension bridges. The bulbous, four-door Chevy lacks air conditioning, but we are cool enough with the windows down. Gas is seventy-five cents a gallon, and five barbeque sandwiches at the Big Pig cost two fifty. Of course, in Philadelphia, a poor man's feast awaits.

"What is the name of that song, again, Mr. Paul? Mr. Paul?"

"What was that?" His hands fly to the hospital bed rails. His head jerks to the left, his eyes are wide and his body stiff.

"I don't know...what did it look like?"

"You saw it...what was it?" He looks anxiously toward the window, gripping both rails tightly.

"I didn't really get a good look, Mr. Paul. What do you think it was?"

"It's ok...it's gone, now." He leans back on the pillows, his body relaxed. I relax a little and realize that I have been gripping the right side railing of the bed. I pry my hands loose and check the clock. Two thirty a.m. – only a few more hours to go.

He has always been susceptible to fevers, ever since I can remember. Usually they are accompanied by horrible leg cramps and only last for a day or two, but this fever is different. He is in the I.C.U. at Baldwin County Hospital after five days in isolation with a fever of one hundred and five. It took three days to grow the culture that confirmed the diagnosis of M.R.S.A. – a staph infection he apparently contracted in the hospital when they performed his knee replacement surgery. He has been out of his mind for almost a week. We have watched him around the clock, my Mom, my brother, my sisters, nieces, nephews, aunts, uncles, friends, anyone who can keep him entertained and in bed so the nurses won't strap him down again. He cries when they strap him down.

So far tonight, we have been to my uncle's farm in Philadelphia,

Mississippi, to my other uncle's house in Pensacola, Florida, to someone named Charley's house in Georgia, and to the Armory in Mobile. That trip was for my Grandmother, dead now for over twenty years. She wanted to go see wraslin' and it was her birthday. Mr. Paul says she had a good time.

He won't sleep. He wants to get out of the bed and go home. I have pretended to bring the car around three times tonight, but we had to wait for Mama to bring his wallet before he could check out, so we're still here. I have managed to keep him in bed, waiting for Mama. Of course, she is at home asleep (I hope) and will not return for several hours, but Mr. Paul takes my word for it and waits patiently. For about five minutes. Then we take off on another trip.

I keep thinking I don't want to remember him like this. I keep thinking he must get better, get healthy again. At 83, that's not really likely, but I can hope.

He's survived the 63rd Infantry's "Blood and Fire" campaign of World War II, retired from Scott Paper Company with arthritis and asbestosis, lost several feet of colon to cancer, had his prostate liquefied by radiation, and is currently being unrealistically optimistic about his liver cancer, but I still can't get used to the idea of him dying.

We've never really been close, he and I. We have had our moments, our camaraderie of Monday night football, and our inside jokes, but when I refer to him as Mr. Paul, that feels more right than "Daddy" ever did. It's not his fault – he gave his life to raise five children, and never complained. He worked seven-day-backup in the number two bleach plant at Scott Paper Company until it became Kimberly Clark, for a grand total of thirty seven years, worked overtime and holidays, missed baseball games, football games, birthday parties, proms and graduations, and rarely said *"I love you."*

When he seems himself, we talk about things, little things like who's making his over-weight beagle Freckles dance for her peppermints – that's the only exercise she gets. We touch on big things – my recent divorce, my nephew's diagnosis of Soft Tissue Sarcoma, Mama's bout with breast cancer – but he keeps slipping in and out of the present, so whatever we say is simply words loitering in the antiseptic air. I smile when he chats up the nurses – lying there in his open-backed gown, cracking jokes, flirting a little when he forgets where he is, telling me how we need to be sure to tip these waitresses for the fine job they're doing, asking for refills of his coffee. They check his vitals, make sure his IV and other tubes are still in place – they laugh and talk to him – they enjoy having a patient who seems to be enjoying himself. It's smiles all around in Room 302.

There's a question hanging in the back of my mind, held in place by guilt, but growing larger and larger by degrees as I refuse to acknowledge it. It was formed one summer day when I was about twelve, like Pandora opening Mr. Paul's foot locker – it is a question only for him. Tucked inside some papers, hidden under his uniform, there were photographs; black and white with serrated edges, faded images of a war he refused to discuss; thin corpses stacked haphazardly like cordwood underneath the Dachau sign, uniformed buddies arm in arm smiling through their fear, a young Mr. Paul standing next to a young woman.

At first glance, it appears to be one of those photographs staged in the old studios; a backdrop of a vineyard trellising off into infinity, a man and a woman standing in front of a low stone wall, he in uniform and she in a flowered dress. She has dark hair curled in a simple fall that frames her face, and she wears low-heeled, strapped pumps. There is something incredibly familiar about her – something about the hair or the eyes or the mouth – she looks like Mama, and yet she doesn't. Of course, she can't be Mama because she and Mr. Paul are the same height. (Mama takes after her father, Papa Lee – tall and broad shouldered – taller than Mr. Paul.) I take the photo to the living room.

"Ask your Father," Mama nods toward Mr. Paul on the other side of the room. He is watching a baseball game on TV, oblivious to us. I walk up next to him and wait to be noticed. In a moment, he turns to me and frowns. I hold out the photograph.

What passes between my parents in the next moments can only be described as low grade electricity – sparks flying from Mama's eyes, dumb fear tensing Mr. Paul's face, the hair on my arm standing on end, a slow sizzle crawling up my spine.

"Ask your Mother," he mumbles, turning back to the game.

I look at Mama – the sparks expire and her eyes go dull. I walk back to her, the photo held out like an offering. She glances at it and makes a *"humph"* sound.

"She's your namesake." Mama frowns. She glances at Mr. Paul, who is very attentively watching his ballgame. She will volunteer no more. I

54

finally give up and walk away.

Mama gave me my first name, but she let Mr. Paul pick my middle name. I have always known there was something strange about the name my father gave me, because every time my Mom yelled at me using my full name she would bite my middle name in half, just like a snapping turtle would a big minnow. This woman in the flowered dress gave me my name. That is all I know about her.

I have been patient about it, asking a question here and there over the years, but people take their pasts very personally, sometimes – regardless of the fact that what they possessively call "their" past is not just theirs, but is also the property of those with whom they shared it – some of it is even a matter of public record. History is a vineyard neglected and tended by everyone at once, everyone planting and pruning and harvesting, everyone minding what each one thinks of as "their" property. When the harvests pile up and the back begins to bow, there are always plenty of gardeners eager to tend another person's plot. Old gardeners love to talk about "their" vineyard.

I learned that my parents very nearly did not get married, thanks to the guile of my grandmother, who did not care for my mother. I know that the photo was taken in Sicily and that the woman was the daughter of a man who opened his house to the American troops, a man who fed them when their supply lines were cut by the Germans. What I do not know is what she was like, this woman whose name – Americanized, but still her name – is mine. I have waited all my life to know her. Perhaps now is the time.

"Sugar, you ready to go?" Mr. Paul is sitting straight up in bed, looking at me. I have been watching him out of the corner of my eye, as he sat there, his fingers weaving invisible objects, his mouth set in a straight line. He brings his hands to his face, with something stretched between them, grabs the something with his teeth and pulls against it. I know this motion, this series of loops and this twiddling of fingers. I know what he is doing in his mind.

"Think you got enough leaders tied?" I ask, pretending to survey his handiwork.

"Well, if we need more, we'll make more," he nods, stowing the invisible leaders away in an invisible tackle box. He sets the invisible tackle box beside him and cranks the invisible car.

55

"Do you feel lucky?" I ask him.

"Shoot, I always feel lucky when I go fishing... don't mean I'm gonna catch nothing... just means I'm lucky enough to go fishing!"

We laugh and drive down to the Gulf of Mexico, to the public pier at Gulf Shores State Park, he in the bed, me standing beside it. His body is a testament to a life lived in the sun, his tanned skin stretched taut over his bones, every laugh and every frown documented on his leathered face. I think about the trials he's endured, about how he and my mother have survived bad times without ever blaming them on each other. Over fifty years they've worked together for the life they wanted – over fifty years yoked together, pulling the same load, completely in step. Theirs is the marriage of hearts and minds, theirs the joy of simple pleasures and the contentment of companionship. They speak in shared silences. I envy them their love. In fact, the only time I remember them crossing words was when I found the photograph.

I watch my father drive his invisible Chevy, his white hair tousled as if by the wind, his eyes bright and his smile genuine. From his motions and expressions, I can almost hear the traffic on the causeway, junkers and pickemups rattling along with poles and buckets in the back, voices scolding an alligator across the road, horns shouting *"hurryup – there's fish waiting to be caught."* He turns his invisible wheel toward the south and I smell the salt, hear the laughter of sea gulls, feel the crunch of oyster shells under the wheels. He brings his car to a stop and pulls up a hand brake. He frowns. Something doesn't feel right.

"Mr. Paul?"

Like a sleepwalker, he looks around the room, wide-eyed and blind, lost in his hospital bed. I consider whether to touch his shoulder. I move until I stand in front of him, where he can see me, if he's in this room.

"Mr. Paul?"

He focuses on me, but he's not looking through his eyes – he's looking inward and my voice has found him there. He stiffens, sitting bolt upright, his arms straight down by his sides, his chin jutting out.

"Sir, yes Sir!" he barks. *"Private First Class Paul, Sir, reporting for orders."*

"Private Paul, do you know where you are?"

I have learned how to play this mind game. He will lead me

through this scenario if I handle it properly. And, if I handle it properly, it will end just as suddenly as it began, disappearing back into his memory where it belongs, no harm done. If I screw up, he will get upset, and the nurses will come. The nurses don't play games.

"*Sir, yes, Sir! We're in Sicily, Sir. At zero five hundred hours we move out. All trucks are loaded, all materials accounted for, Sir!*"

Did he say Sicily?

Of all the trips we've taken tonight, we've never been to Sicily. I wonder if this is some sort of mental connection we have made, a suggestion from my unconscious mind answered by his? Is that possible? Apparently, I am his commanding officer. I could ask him where he took that photograph. I could demand to know who the woman in the photo is. I mean, she could be a spy or a Nazi sympathizer, you never know. He would have to tell me – wouldn't he?

After all, what harm would it do? When this is all over, he probably won't remember any of it. Considering the medication they have injected into him, and the effects of the fever, later this may all be a surrealistic blur – the realities of his experience hopelessly blended with the fantasies. Whatever he tells me will be mine, alone.

Suddenly, I am a child reaching for a strawberry – one of my grandfather's prize strawberries. Mr. Lee is a gentleman farmer: every year when he plants crops, he selects plants to raise for his own amusement, his little experiments in horticulture, forbidden to anyone but him. Mind you, I could pick anything in his garden, any time I wanted – except these berries. There are rows and rows of other berries, perfectly good berries, but I only want these. I reach out to pluck the biggest, ripest one. A tall, broad-shouldered shadow falls over me. I freeze. The shadow shakes its head.

"*Character is a funny thing,*" Papa Lee rumbles, his voice like summer thunder, low and distant, "*you can only prove you have it when no one is looking.*"

After a moment, the shadow moves away.

Mr. Paul hasn't moved. He sits bolt upright in his hospital bed, in a backless gown, at attention, awaiting his orders. Of the soldier that he was, little remains except this nobility of spirit, this insane bravery. He seems so small now – somehow, so far away. It's almost as if he is leaving us, ounce by ounce, organ by organ, in parts and pieces, little by little.

It's almost as if God is using sleight of hand – now you see him, now you don't, or not as much, anyway. But he is a fighter – his life must be wrestled from him – he won't give it up easily. He deserves respect. And gratitude. And love.

My father, white-haired, wasted by disease, arthritic and asthmatic from thirty-seven years at the paper mill, is still waiting for his orders, still ready to lay down his life for his country, still ready to protect the ones he loves.

"Private Paul?" I ask, as brusquely as I can muster.

"Sir, yes Sir!"

"Get some sleep, you've got a big day tomorrow."

"Sir, yes Sir!"

He falls out and into sleep, as ordered – my father, an old soldier at rest.

I watch him for a long, long time.

I Sing the Soul Electric

And if the body were not the Soul, what is the Soul?
"I Sing the Body Electric," **Walt Whitman**

Hallelujah!
> for green mist afternoons,
> for clouds so swollen
they lay their pregnant bellies on the ground.

Hosannas!
> Life primordial is born,
> shimmies to thunder rumbling
basso profundo in the psychic air.

Fioritura!
> Leaves and blossoms tremble,
> all bow down,
supinate, genuflecting.

Sotto voce!
> my tingling tongue,
> my humming heart,
my pulsing eardrums.

Come, Heaven!
> come angelic flame,
> in the name of all things
sentient, come!

Vibrato!
> Strike the tuning fork of life!
> Make all that lives, vibrate,
for all that vibrates, sings.

Bel Canto!
> Sing to the thrumming
> pulse of summer – *Hallelujah!* –
My soul, electric,
> > *SING!*

Watermelons at Hazel's

I am the white devil, the slaver, the traitor.
Being Southern is my original sin.
The deeds of my fathers are visited upon me.
My inheritance is dust, gone with the wind.

Like every child, I was born with Original Sin,
but Christ Jesus died to set me free –
or was it Scarlett O'Hara in *"Gone With the Wind?"*
I keep forgetting…who am I supposed to be?

Yes, Jesus died to set me free –
but He never saw *"Birth of A Nation,"*
and – sorry – but a hoop-skirted debutante just ain't me,
more like a honky white cracker full of indignation.

Where the Hell did they film *"Birth of a Nation?"*
They don't have that many white sheets at J.C. Penney.
OK – I'm a honky white cracker full of indignation,
but have you seen what the media has done to me?

I buy my pastel sheets at J.C. Penney,
watermelons at Hazel's, sweet corn in season,
and if the media chooses to demonize me,
I wouldn't mind if I had given them reason.

So, I will eat watermelons and grow wise in season,
because if being Southern is my Original Sin,
and if being the child of my father is treason –
then my inheritance, like dust, is gone with the wind.

P.T. PAUL

In Pelican We Trust

Pelican is my copilot,
I shall not wander.

He accompanies me across the Bayway,
his wings spread wide, riding
on my wake, gliding side by side.

I shall not hurry.

His is the wisdom
of sunsets on pier posts,
the patience of tides,
he will outwait the fishermen,
he will weather like creosote,
he will abide.

Pelican is my copilot,
I shall not question.

His is the zen
of jubilees and drought,
he teaches me the fallacy
of bird in hand or
fish in beak.

I will not be weak.

My own life, soft and
comforting, is an illusion –
my fortune is circumstance,
not holy writ.

I shall rejoice and be glad in it.

And I shall live like the pelican,
perching on each day
with my face to the wind,
awaiting the how and the when,
for the plunge
and the occasional, simple epiphany.

"Where My Skies Are So Blue"*

Sometimes the sky foams up like the ocean
With clouds of white bubbles banking the horizon
Evanescent as daydreams, tides of thunder
Ending with the shout and whisper of rain,
Tides receding into darkness to gather again.

Heavy with moisture, summer shuffles along
On flip flops, striking heat lightning
More flash than fire, a bioluminescent
Emission at night, clouds like fireflies in flight.

August ends only man's designs,
Like children not ready to leave the beach,
Ascending clouds hang before falling again,
Bathwater afternoons thick enough to swim through,
Anthems of bullfrogs celebrate saturation,
Man is just a tourist in the summer storm cycle –
A fish out of water in an aquatic world.

*"*Sweet Home Alabama,*" Lynyrd Skynyrd

P.T. PAUL

How to Peel an Orange

He takes an orange in his left hand –
the top one, as they are all equally desirable – the knife in his right.

It is his favorite knife, the paring knife with the wooden handle.
He grips the handle with his lower three fingers,
wraps his thumb from the other direction,
lays his index finger along the back of the blade.

Two rotations – two scores – from top to bottom – just a flick of the wrist –
the peel falls off in four pieces. He holds the naked orange out like a trophy.
"There," he says.

I approach the bowl of oranges with a joy akin to wonder.
I examine them all for ripeness, firmness, orange-ness.
I select one and bring it to my face.
I close my eyes and smell orange.

I take my father knife from the drawer, the one that is metal from tip to tip.
No wooden handle to ruin in the dishwasher. No pretension, just knife.
It fits my hand like a memory.

I sit on the couch, paper napkin in my lap. I examine my orange.
I marvel in its nubbie, dimpled, oily skin. I smell it again.
I turn it navel up. We have this feature in common: it's an innie - just like mine.
I slide the knife just below the skin and begin to turn the orange
counterclockwise.

*"We were only an hour and a half from Florida, down Hwy 112
over the Styx River -- at the Charon Crossing," I explain.
"We had winters in Alabama, once snow at Mardi Gras,
but we were only semi-tropical -- we could not grow oranges."*

The peel tries to recoil itself, like a lazy snake. I let it hang.
It dangles and straightens, only the very end of it still round.

*"They lived in Pensacola. My aunt was from Bonifay,
It was named for her people. Dad Bonifay lived with them.
He peeled my orange when I was too young to be trusted with knives.
He told me about Florida Indians and played ragtime piano by ear.
I sat on his lap. He called me 'Shug'."*

63

To Live & Write in Dixie

I slice off the butt end of the orange – now the peel has two endings.
I recoil it in my lap on the paper napkin, a snake with two heads.
"We slept late in Pensacola, ate Krispie Kreme doughnuts for breakfast
with orange juice – all we wanted – in thin metal cups that had been in the freezer.
We crunched icebergs of orange pulp. We went to the beach every day."

I slip the knife under the white sheath that protects the orange.
It tears away like cotton batting, makes a small sound
like thick, soaked fabric ripping. I stack it like quilt squares.

"One night I walked out onto the porch because I could not breathe.
All the doors and windows were open, but there was no breeze.
The box fans blew their own engine heat around the room.
The air hung like the Spanish Moss – a thick, immobile, organic thing.
My aunt clicked from channel to channel on the black and white TV.
There was snow on every channel. My uncle held a small radio to his ear."

I lift the edge of the fiber polar cap, grab with my fingernails and pull.
The capsules of orange pulp that surround the stem remind me
of pomegranate seeds. The fleshy core pops up like an exclamation point.

"The storm attacked the house like an insane washer woman,
slinging tree limbs on the porch with Spanish Moss trailing,
flinging acorns with deadly aim, splashing rain like dirty water slops
from a bottomless washtub, screaming from every direction at once,
a rampage of wind and water and whatever would fly."

I slide my thumb into the core of the orange and pull the sections apart.

"The next day, Daddy came for us. Mama had lost the baby."

I peel every section of orange. I do not eat the skins. I eat sections whole.
They burst, pulp bombs like orange suns exploding in my mouth.
Sweet beyond understanding. Sweet like Jesus's voice in the Bible.

"We never got to stay with my aunt like that again. Dad Bonifay died.
No one else could play ragtime piano. We got oranges at the farmers market."

The orange is now a coiled snake of peeling, stacked quilt squares of white flesh,
piled slivers of loose skin, and a radiating sun of sweetness in my stomach.
I hold the napkin of orange carnage out to him like an offering. I smile.

"There," I say.

Quiltestry
(From "Quilts" by Nikki Giovanni)

My aunts flock to the meeting hall,
their hands needled,
their backs bowed to the quilting frame.
Their names are Mother,
Sister, Friend.

They stitch up raveled
sleeves of sleep,
they Stygian peep
of So-and-So
and sew.

Widow Birds, they speak of husbands,
lost wedding bands,
their hands are praying
*"dear Lord, my soul,
to keep."*

They are the gods forgotten –
they bred, they birthed, they said,
"Don't forget…" but fledglings
always fly.

And I? I play no part in this
quiltestry –
my needle holds
less sturdy thread.

Instead,
I write of Widow Birds,
hope someone will find my words,
wrap memories around them

and be warm.

Joe Willy, You Done Busted Up My Record

Why'd you do it, Joe Willy? What was it to you?
Winner of Super Bowls, star quarterback
of the Jets? Of the Crimson Tide? Of my childhood?

You know, you were a god to me?
Apollo, Zeus, Joe Willy: the Greek god of the spiral –
your thunderbolt unerring in its flight –
you Hermes of Monday Night – you broke my heart
when you stumbled out of the pocket
on your busted-up knees.
You were beautiful to me.

At Vigor High School, that breeding ground for quarterbacks,
Mr. Murphy in Algebra patted my hand – he could not be bothered
to teach math to me, since I only needed to be able
to count to twenty eight.
And girls can't throw spirals.

You left Beaver Falls for Tuscaloosa.
I took a job in the tissue mill at Scott.
We both stumbled through our freshman and sophomore years.
You got better and lettered in football,
then went long with the pros on the strength of your perfect spiral.
I got tired and took an "Mrs." degree.

And just when I thought I had done something,
you came back to Alabama to smash my "longest-return" record.
Your promise brought you back. Mine, too –
plus a failed marriage and every boss at every entry-level dead-end job
who ever said "I CAN'T pay you more,
because you don't have a degree..."
Why'd you do it to me, Joe Willy?

Once again, your arm went back, you looked down the field,
standing god-like on granite knees –
you went long academically – and stomped me.
I guess we both had to do it, didn't we?

Hell, I'm proud you done busted up my record, Joe Willy.
And you're still beautiful to me.

P.T. PAUL

It's How You Play The Game

"Come on down, forget your care,
 Come on down, you'll find me there..."

"Tuxedo Junction" croons to the crack
 of a Louisville Slugger
as the right fielder hoofs it in the bright May sunshine –
 but that ball is over the Burma Shave sign...and gone.

It's the 2004 "Rickwood Field Classic,"
 Sloss Industries still trails by three
and U.S. Steel will not give it up,
 but the pups are hot and the beer ice cold.

"Fire" Trucks is there, signing score cards and balls,
 and, sitting right in front of us,
Joe Weaver eats a snow cone.

"Excuse me, Sir... Mr. Weaver, can I have your autograph?"

His smile stretches the bronze leather of his cheeks,
 but the hand he holds out does not falter.

"What was it like? Back then? Did U.S. Steel really win?"

 Just a blink and the smile fades –
"That was a long time ago, you know?
 A lot has happened since then..."

You can read it in his face, like a roadmap of history;
 the Great Depression, World War II,
 a league where *"only the ball was white,"**
sleeping in the back seat of a car in the "Whites Only" hotel parking lot,
 shining shoes, or carrying bags at the train station
 like Leroy "Satchel" Paige, or walking barefoot to the ballpark
to borrow shoes in which to play, like "Shoeless Joe" Jackson.

Joe Wheeler might agree with "Cool Papa" Bell,
 considered the fastest man ever to play professional baseball,
who died on Social Security and a "quiet stipend"
 from the baseball commissioner's office,

when he said that he was not born too early,
"they just opened the doors too late."

He would certainly agree that the greatest obstacle to overcome is hate.

But, this is his moment, so you intrude, break the spell –
    "Like they say,
        it's not really about whether you win..."

"That's right..." he nods, turns back to the field
    where young men who might be his grandsons
    wear his uniform and run his bases –
this man who is a legend from a time when survival was the only trophy.
    Finally, he smiles, again.

That's how you play the game.

"Tuxedo Junction," Erskine Hawkins & Bill Johnson, lyrics by Buddy Feyne
* "Only the Ball Was White" Robert Peterson, 1970

P.T. PAUL

that funky music

mobile ain't a young man's town,
papermills and rusted malls,

streets that can't recall their names
and, over all,
                    spanish moss
that much-loved parasite

but, once a year, a young man's game
rolls like jubilee down gov'ment street

scoots boots, strolls, boogies and bops
like sparks from a cd in a microwave

play that funky music, white boy*,
roll us back to nineteen ninety whatever

follow the saints to bienville square
help us refugees find each other

snatch plastic jewels from thin air
coins that won't buy anything

quick, while the moonpie owns the sky
lay down that boogie

and play that funky music
till we die.

* *"Play That Funky Music"*– Wild Cherry, 1976

Psychic Tears

*"Psychic weeping is not known to occur as a normal function
in any animal other than man."*
(Crying: The Mystery of Tears by William H. Frey, Ph.D. 1985)

Darwin, that Adam of Galapagos,
was told by the keepers of Indian elephants at the London Zoo
that those pachyderms swaying from side to side on shackled legs
would sometimes weep for sorrow.

It was once thought that aquatic creatures like seals and sea otters
cried to release excess salt from their bodies,
and that we, so lately sprung from the primordial ooze,
cried for that reason, too.

Dian Fossey reported in *"Gorillas in the Mist"*
that the silver-backed monarchs also cried,
but, perhaps she identified too much
with that species' plight.

In fact, all creatures with complex eyes cry –
basal tears for lubrication, reflective tears as reactions –
but man is said to be the only animal
that cries psychic tears for grief or joy.

You can believe this if you choose.

But, I have watched my father's four-footed friend
stand in the spot where his life ended
and drop tears on the carpet while her howl was answered
by some wild thing in the thoughtless woods.

And, I was there when her search for him ended in the hollow
where she laid her head on the cap he lost to his last storm,
and waited out her last breath, like any well-trained hunting dog,
for her master to come back and take her home.

Take This Bread

He did NOT say,

"genetically reengineer the plant
so that it is resistant to disease,
     assuming that this alteration
     will not harm those who consume it –

treat the crop with poisons
to kill those insects that would feed on it,
     assuming that those poisons
     will know whom they are meant to harm –

harvest the crop with large machinery
that wastes fossil fuels,
     assuming that these fuels do not harm the environment
     and will never be depleted –

use the excess grain as collateral
to hold less fortunate countries hostage,
     assuming that the status quo
     is righteous and eternal –

process the grain into food that has a shelf life
commensurate to the lifestyle of the moment,
     assuming that food is your birthright
     and can be taken for granted –

and, finally, waste the food
that you have produced,
     assuming that science and technology
     will always produce more –

        and, all THESE things do
           in remembrance of Me..."

Ode to A Hummingbird

We have planted red salvia for you,
purchased orange-flowered Cape Honey Suckle,
and tangled yellow-blossomed Carolina Jasmine.
We have filled plastic feeders
with ruby sugar nectar,
hung them from the eaves of the house,
waited by the window.

When will the spring winds
blow you back to our flowered porch?
When will we catch a glimpse
of your scarlet, jeweled throat,
the green blur of wings moving
faster than the eye can follow?

We have heard the stories of sailors
drifting on your flight path
whose rigging rang out
like a million small bells,
suddenly hung like a jeweled necklace
for a few breathless moments
while you rested from your swarm
across the Gulf of Mexico.

Your scouts have been spotted,
your advance guard of males
who search for
the nectar flowers,
trumpet blossoms,
honey suckle,
morning glories,
for the ruby sugar-water feeders,
for salvia, for jasmine,
and we wait for your return
like we wait for hurricanes,
prepared, anxious, wondering
what the next wind
will bring.

P.T. PAUL

Sister To The River Of Forgetfulness

iced tea crawling over sugar sand
sister to the river of forgetfulness
even scrub pines take your tannins
in needle-fine sips

in August you cool us
chill our watermelons in your icy clutch
where wandering roots double up
retreating from your numbing touch

you knew my grandfather, took his breath
when he swung and dropped like a silver spoon
into your deceptive amber depths
I may see you soon

come some weary moon
ask Uncle Levi to dowse for my grave
slip beneath Clear Springs Cemetery while cicadas croon
sail your eternal stream, unlost, unsaved

inheritance

never was much good to fight it
creams and bleaches, curses.

mama said   *don't make no never mind*

scratched at her scars.
freckles, blotches, sure as sin,
bruises ripen like eggplant,
                like tomatoes,
                like scuppernongs.

we are speckled butterbean people,
crackled enamel washtub people,
fawn-spotted, coffee with cream people,
pale as yard eggs, dark as topsoil,
leathered, parchment walking scrolls.

doctor says   *stay out of the sun.*

bible says   *man's days are numbered.*

sunup yokes the mule to the plow,
sun goes down behind the butterbeans,
sweat begets watermelons, corn, potatoes,
sleep rides on the back of the thunderstorm,
that black bear still lays up in the hollow
death rides us down from the inside

connect the blemishes,
spell the word   *family*

Everyday

His absence is a presence in our everyday,
our every word, our workaday world,

hanging like his hat
on the hook of our consciousness,

less than his fragrance
on the coat that he wore,

solid as the plaque he made
for the front door;

his voice carved in pine darkening over time
to a false patina of permanence.

This is the fence he wrapped around the garden,
large-holed wire – insincere in its threat –

flowered by flights of morning glories,
bent inward by the insistence of deer.

If he were here, he would plant clover for them
in the patch where his gaze could fall

like lamplight from the window –
his joy walking spindly-legged in the moonlight,

drifting to the greens
where they were never meant to be.

Dear me, could you blame them
when the frost brought the sweetness up?

Even the beagle pup observes from a distance,
roused from sleep

by footsteps soft as raindrops,
hypnotized by their moonless eyes.

Constellatio Avi
(Latin: *"Grandfathers' Constellation"*)

Somewhere in that summer sky there should be a plowman
glistening of sweat starlets against the black bottom land of night,
straining throughout eternity to turn the perfect furrow
that terminates in the system "Bountiful Harvest"
           and brings him peace, at last.

Alabama summer nights flow past without awakenings
of greed for more than stains the spoon or pulls the covers tight –
a farmer's life, a farmer's wife, both laid beneath the moon.

His legacy? a lineage traced in dust from east to west
and best recalled on porch steps when evening breezes squall
           that August loved them best of all.

I have his aquiline features, my brother has his knife,
but for the life of me I can't recall what happened to the bullwhip
that snapped the heifers' eyes wide and quickened
her homeward two-step.

(Remember; stones laid one upon the other never care for that design
and signs of winter sought on Wooly Bears
are like runes read in Solstice skies; a figment of your mind.)

Listen – his voice rolls around in the rain barrel
whose staves tremble on rotting ribs,
he stomps the quake of cumulus mountains
that tumbles down the crashing rain –
           he lives again.

Somewhere in that summer sky there should be a plowman
glistening of sweat starlets against the black bottom land of night,
straining throughout eternity to turn that perfect furrow
that terminates in the system *"Bountiful Harvest"*
           and brings him peace at last.

Somewhere in that summer sky there *must* be a plowman –
           his eyes sparkling the patient blue of memory.

Focus Four

The Living, Breathing South

Excerpt from NY Daily News, Q&A with Gen. Wesley Clark:

Q: *And what is Clark's reaction to former Vermont Gov. Howard Dean's pandering comment that that he, Dean, wants the votes of Southerners, i.e. "guys with Confederate flags in their pickup trucks"?*

A: *"Well, he shouldn't have said those things. I think all Americans – and this is a joke! – all Americans, even if they're from the South and 'stupid,' should be represented."*

Dems Can't Help Themselves[Rod Dreher]
National Review, The Corner, Sunday, November 09, 2003

"Stereotypes are always rooted in some truth."

Tom Hanchett, Historian at the Levine Museum
Pop Culture, Y'all come: Exhibit Focuses on Southern Stereotypes
Leigh Dyer,McClatchy Newspapers, Sept. 20, 2007

Bloodlines

Angora goats nibble daintily on serpentine kudzu,
whose teacup white blossoms hold dreams up to moonshine,
then strangles other vines, like verdigris muscadines
and the grape-cluster fairy-flowered variegated wisteria.
Nature favors the aggressive: those green, grasping bloodlines
whose blooms search the moon for the runes of their ancestors.

Vervain and Viper's Budloss were used by my ancestors
to cure bites of serpents that hid in the kudzu.
Transplants, also, we traced our own tangled bloodlines
by granite slabs that glowed phosphorescent in moonshine.
We planted, and repented of sky climbing wisteria
and sweetened biscuits with jellied essence of muscadines.

Others discovered distilled secrets of muscadine,
but we were kept sober by the sins of our ancestors.
Instead, we sipped iced tea beneath bowers of wisteria
and cursed the crop-claiming advance of the kudzu.
Somewhere in the intoxicating glow of moonshine
we wove myths of our ancestors and tangled our bloodlines.

In all countries, we worship the gods of our bloodlines;
in Provencal, they lift a glass to the sweet god of muscadines.
In Dixie, they worship the gold god of moonshine
that ties them to this verdant land of their ancestors,
where homesteads untended are swallowed by kudzu,
while ancient oaks bow their heads to the god of wisteria.

Wreathe roots with fallen leaves to best grow wisteria
and glory in the variegated bouquets of its bloodline,
just as someone in Kyoto tends to their kudzu
with the same care that someone in Provance shows their muscadines.
These roots that were planted and cultivated by ancestors
grace our slumber with wisteria and kudzu scented moonshine.

Eden was a garden once dreamed of in moonshine
where sunrise was scented by sky climbing wisteria,
at least, that was the fairy tale told by our ancestors
whose headstones still silently brag of their bloodlines.

Down nameless hollows have fallen now feral muscadines,
pursued and subdued by unloved kudzu.

What dreams did unwanted kudzu have in moonshine?
Tangled images of lost homelands, like muscadine and wisteria?
Such dreams are bloodlines that tie us to ancestors.

Blakeley Forgets

You may find telling tracks; fat-bottomed parenthesis
made by the hooves of white tail deer, fat and skinny W's
of turkey and heron, five-fingered palm prints of raccoon
and black bear, and the sand wave S's of the reticulated kind.

Blakeley belongs to the moment, to the sweet gum and cedar,
to the pine and Formosa, to the scrub oak and magnolia,
to the gossip of squirrels, to the cooing of pigeons,
to the *hiss*per of a ground rattler, to the roaring forced march
of the Tensaw River flowing to its bivouac in Mobile Bay.

Once upon a misery, these earthworks were piled up,
oaks laid down, bridges built and burned. Footpaths swelled
into causeways across rivulets, brambles were trampled,
gray flannel snags surrendered to *"wait-a-minute"* vines,
flesh and blood were sanctified in the cold fire
of black powder and cast-iron solid shot.

Blakeley has forgotten prayers muttered in muddy trenches,
can no longer recall trails laid down by cannon wheels
or shallow burrows dug by desperate hands. This land
belongs to no man, espouses no creed, holds no truths self-evident
except the sudden scream of a red-tailed hawk's fall,
or the settling of the faster mourning dove
on a branch above the meadow.

Extinct In Alabama
(A Found Poem)

A normal rate is a few species
    per million years –
a mass extinction is when
    that doubles.

In the last 600 million years,
    we have lost

    the Carolina Parakeet
    the Passenger Pigeon
    the Leafshell Clam
    the Tennessee Rifleshell Clam

    and uncounted unknown others.

These species were crowded out,
    hunted out,
    poisoned out,
    polluted out,
by their shared natural enemy
    and nemesis

    man.

In my lifetime – in yours –
    more species may disappear
than were lost 65 million years ago
    in that anonymous
    mass extinction.

Among them, *please God,* let there be
    the lineage
    of Jim Crow

and the tree that bore the strange,
    muted fruit
    of our childhood.

Keep Dancing

Eugene Walter was the first to document
their gangly limbs gyrating as if they led
the Second Line, their umbrellas pumping time
to a zydeco serenade – *"oh, when the Saints
go marching in!"* – curling tails held aloft,
paws padding like tap shoes across the page.

In his age, he saw loblollies fall
and factories rise from the shores of Mobile Bay,
shopping malls splay themselves
across acrid swamps, gunmetal gray ghosts
haunt rivers leading to the Gulf of Mexico,
Eugene had seen prosperity, wars and hurricanes come and go.

In Minamata, Japan, people noticed felines behaving oddly –
called it *"The Cat Dancing Disease"* – thought nothing of it
until crows fell from the sky and fish floated
white bellied and white eyed in Minamata Bay,
a mercuric jubilee tide flowing to the Shiranui Sea,
a five-year old girl the first human to join the dance.

Eugene, that *"Untidy Pilgrim,"* had been far beyond
the shores of Mobile Bay, had been a minor
luminary in the City of Light, returning to help found
the opera and symphony, but his axiom *"when in danger,
fill the bathtub with Jim Beam and swim your way to safety"*
could not save him from the malaise that had settled on society.

"The Cat Dancing Disease" continued for thirty years,
as Minamata searched for the source of her suffering.
Mobile repented of her greed in far less time,
jubilees resumed their barometric schedule,
and Eugene followed Joe Cain to Church Street Cemetery
in a coffin scrawled with farewells from friends.

And, one might think that's where the story ends –
but greed is a tapeworm in the gut of society,
prosperity is never measured in poets or cats,
and the toxins are within us, planning their choreography.
So, find the Jim Beam, fill the bathtub if you must, but remember –
if you do join the line, like Eugene told us, *"No matter what, keep dancing!"*

In The Sahara Of The Bozart
(A knee-jerk response to "The Sahara of the Bozart" by H.L. Mencken)

It's too bad, H.L., that you weren't standing outside that anonymous
Southern redneck bar when Neil Young, that frail Canadian flower,
got his ass kicked and decided, in retaliation, to hightail it home
and write his sulking rock diatribes "Southern Man" and "Alabama."

And it's a shame, H.L., that you wrote "The Sahara of the Bozarts"
before Lynyrd Skynyrd (those redneck Floridians) retaliated with
"Sweet Home Alabama" and put Neil in his place with those
erudite lyrics *"A Southern man don't need him around, anyhow."*

I guess you will just have to be content with the knowledge that you
inspired the New Agrarians, that Wendell Berry may have written
"The Mad Farmer Manifesto" in answer to your disparaging remarks,
that a whole new generation of writers took up the gauntlet to put you

in your place, in true Southern knee-jerk style, as you might say. *"Obviously,
it is impossible for intelligence to flourish in such an atmosphere,"* you
famously harangued, as evidenced by the poetry of your chosen example,
"the last bard of Dixie," J. Gordon Coogler, who wrote *"Alas, for the South!*

Her books have grown fewer – She never was much given to literature." You mourned
him, H.L., as that rarest of breed, *"almost as rare as an oboe-player,
a dry-point etcher or a metaphysician"* – a poet from Dixie. So we shall not speak
of James Dickey, H.L., of his belief that *"there is a poet —or a kind of poet —*

buried in every human being," because, as he himself said, *"I came to poetry with no
particular qualifications."* You would dismiss him, H.L., as easily as you would
dismiss me, since humility is not a virtue you aspire to, but we may have found a
truth we can adhere to – a Southern man don't need *you* around, anyhow.

Jubilee

Pearl of a moon hung on its side
strung into lesser pearls by the tide
tide lines overlapping, slapping,
insolent and sullen, slovenly
and sere.

    We are drawn here.

Oil of ocean,
grit of sand,
night shows its face like the back of a hand –
there is wind,
but it is insincere.

First a crab, then several,
thoughtless and frightened,

    easy to catch.

The rest in a jumble,
spat out like breakfast
when the stomach turns,

wide-eyed as burn victims,
fins flapping,
tails slapping,
mouths snapping at the air,

and we are there
like thieves,
like undertakers,
anonymous in the darkness,
scooping up

    the trembling dead.

The moon hides its face.

The ocean turns its tide.

The Perfect Curtsey

Desiree slips on her lacey, filigree gloves,
straightens her taffeta-lined open-crowned hat, twirls
her matching organza and taffeta parasol.

She has chosen the color and pattern of her dress,
has marked her calendar and packed her suitcase,
has practiced her swaying walk, her demur nods, her careful turns.

Her Blackberry is on *"silent"* in the pocket of her pantaloons,
her smile is at the ready to respond to any language,
a pastel ambassador, she is poised, self-assured.

Like her hoops, there is a steel will that shapes her actions,
a determination to succeed that has informed her life,
and from which she will forge the future she has dreamed.

No one in her family has ever worn a hoopskirt, twirled
a parasol, collapsed like falling flowers at summer's end
into a fuchsia puddle to execute the perfect curtsey – no one.

She is a contrast, a contradiction, her honey-brown skin
brought into bloom by her fuchsia frills, a modern Southern Belle,
the great-great-great-great-great-granddaughter of slaves.

Today, she will pose on the steps of an antebellum mansion,
her hoop skirts linking her to a mythical past – a marketers' dream –
and to the future these moments will bring.

To those who see only symbols of oppression she answers,
"To honor those whose lives were not of their choosing,"
and it is to them that she makes her perfect curtsey.

To Be Southern
(After Emily Dickinson's *"I like to see it lap the miles"*)

To be Southern is to be intimate with hurricanes,
to recite the names Camille, Frederic, Georges,
Ivan and Katrina
as if one knew their dams and sires,
as if Miss Emily's bolting steed –
docile and omnipotent –
freed its feral cousin wind-kind from anonymity.

Their smaller brothers are said
to roar like iron horses –
Boanerges – 'sons of thunder'
struck from anvil clouds, unnamed
land-locked renegades stomping valleys of debris
to wallow down in,
flint-shod, frothing.

To be Southern is to raise ones head
when summer bellows out its jaws.
Satchmo never blew a note so low –
a horrid, hooting stanza –
weighted down with the melody
of the wind's topographical memory,
twisters fingering the Braille
of shanty,
doublewide,
ranch-style bungalow,
pregnant with homelessness,
riding twisted rails of a train wreck sky,
searching for their lost stable door.

In This Polite Country

It's considered bad luck to be rude to them,
no matter whether they jack up the covers
or mumble under the stairwell
about how Sherman used their grandmother's coverlet
to dry his mud-crusted bay stallion.

And they are everywhere – some of the best hotels
promise sightings like the ducks at the Peabody –
so much for resting in peace.
The best-bred families chuckle and knock back brandy,
sleep with earplugs and Prince Valium.

But, what else is one to do with them,
when they couldn't be routed by artillery,
drank salted well water strained
through scraps of cheese cloth,
developed a taste for acorn mush.

In this lush landscape, in this polite country,
they have rights irrevocable
and eminent domain,
and every evening, when the old days meet Early Times,
the South, like the new moon, rises again.

Something About The Heat

Summer mumbles something about the heat,
sweat falling from her brow.
How is a season supposed to reason
with the heat cooking up such potent stuff
as asphalt after-fragrance dancing on oil-slick fumes
in afternoon olfactory assault on clear blue-eyed summer skies?
It's enough to make any season cry.

Summer mumbles something about the heat
and beats city sky scraper dust from her sheets.
Cracking linen whips, she ripples stale slipstreams
ripping off the top sheet, fitted sheet, mattress cover –
Hell, throw the whole thing over.
Dump dirty laundry and disintegrating moisture pillows,
then billow the sky with fine new percale.
Snap hospital corners of fresh atmosphere –
clear, cool linens to begin again
the bedding of July.

Summer mumbles something about the heat,
flinging undergarments in a heap –
sweat-soaked cottons dumped in the drink,
swirled in agitated circles of tropical complaint,
pumped up and down and all around against islands awash,
flung at last upon the shore of some larger land mass
to drip dry – thermals weave fresh air dainties heavenward;
the latest fashion to die for!

Summer mumbles something about the heat
in fits of sleep that shift constellations in their climb.
Her prime long past, she tosses in dreams
of a star-crossed lover
whose name she will discover in due time.
His sign diametrically opposed, she must suppose
their meeting would quench her fire,
but the fear she lacks will be her undoing and her fall –
for, as she should know, opposites attract.

P.T. PAUL

Some Say

Some say that jazz notes never die,
   they just fly up into the arms of twisted oaks,
snuggle down among the Spanish Moss
  and Mardi Gras beads,

  and feed on funeral dirges,
Second Line Scat and lonesome, heartsick
     lovers blues.

You can hear them when the wind
   winds down Government Street
     chasing some flirtatious moon
into the mouth of Mobile Bay.

They say, *Come and find us, pretty child,*
with your nimble fingers and your supple lips.

Come and whistle us, pick up that horn
your granddaddy played, lay us down

like sorghum sliding down a silver spoon.
Play us, pretty child, play.

  Some say,
that's the voice of the devil! Ain't no music
  lives in the trees.

  Some say, *you gotta work*
for it – give it your life – ain't nothing worthwhile
     comes for free.

  Some say this and some say
that, and I can't say what I believe, but,

sometimes, when the wind blows warm
  down Government Street
and the Spanish Moss rustles in the leaves,

and it's silent as the moon on Mobile Bay,
  something sways,

     something sways.

References

Academy of American Poets, Poets.org.,(2009) Source of James Dickey quotes for "In the Sahara of the Bozarts". http://www.poets.org/poet.php/prmPID/363#

Allexperts.com. (2009) Information about Eugene Walter for "Keep Dancing". http://en.allexperts.com/e/e/eu/eugene_walter.htm

Answers.com. (2009) Information on Jubilees for "The Lesson of Tides" p.2 http://www.answers.com/topic/hypoxia-environmental

Associated Press (2009) *Source of Azalea Trail Maids Remind NAACP Of Slavery* for "The Perfect Curtsey". http://www.wkrg.com/alabama/article/trail_maids_debate/22453/Jan-08-2009_2-40-pm/

Bullock, Mimi. (2008) *Discusses the Pelican Girls, Early History of Mobile* for "The Pelican Girls". http://www.associatedcontent.com/article/1003784/the_story_of_the_pelican_girls.html?cat=37

Dickinson, Emily (1955) *"I like to see it lap the miles"* Complete Poems of Emily Dickinson for "To Be Southern". http://www.americanpoems.com/poets/emilydickinson/585.shtml

Dreher, Rod. (2003) Exerpt from question and answer session with Gen. Wesley Clark, in which stereotypes of Southerners are discussed for Focus Four quote. *Dems Can't Help Themselves*, National Review, The Corner, November 2003 http://corner.nationalreview.com/post/?q=NjNlMmYzOTkyNDBlY2QzZTE2ZDEzMThlM2EwMmNlM2U=

Dyer, Leigh. (2007) Statements about Southern stereotypes for Focus Three quote. *Y'all come: Exhibit Focuses on Southern Stereotypes*, Pop Culture, McClatchy Newspapers, Charlotte, NC. http://www.azcentral.com/ent/pop/articles/0920southernstereotypes0920.html

Historic Blakeley State Park website, (2009) Information used in "Blakeley Forgets". http://new.siteone.com/sites/blakeleypark.com/

Keller, F., *Mississippi River ran backward ???* (2009) Source of anecdotal information on phenomena surrounding earthquakes, columns of flame, etc. for "It Is Written".
http://www.showme.net/~fkeller/quake/mississippi_river_ran_backward.htm

Lavender, Catherine (2001) *D.W. Griffith, The Birth of a Nation* (1915) Source of information for "White Sheets" p.42 and "Watermelons at Hazel's".
http://www.library.csi.cuny.edu/dept/history/lavender/birth.html

Mencken, H.L.(1917) *The Sahara of the Bozart.* Source of information for "In the Sahara of the Bozart". Prejudices, A Selection, Vintage Books, A Division of Random House, N.Y.

Strange, John (2007) *The History of the Mobile Azalea Trail,* Source of information for "The Perfect Curtsey".
http://www.johnstrange.com/edm310summer07/hinds/history.html

Uni, Jun. (2009) Source of information on "Minimata Disease" aka "Disease of the Dancing Cats" for "Keep Dancing".
http://www.unu.edu/unupress/unupbooks/uu35ie/uu35ie0c.htm

Warren, Robert Penn. (1961) An essay discussing the impact of the Civil War. Source of quote for Focus One, p.1 and "Special Field Orders Number Fifteen". The Legacy of the Civil War, University of Nebraska Press, Lincoln.

www.ingramcontent.com/pod-product-compliance
Lightning Source LLC
Chambersburg PA
CBHW031144090426
42738CB00008B/1207